# The Skills of Teaching:

## Lesson Planning Skills

David H. Berenson, Ph.D.
Sally R. Berenson, M.S. Ed.
Robert R. Carkhuff, Ph.D.

CARKHUFF
INSTITUTE
of HUMAN
TECHNOLOGY

Human
Resource
Development
Press

Publishers of Human Technology

D1455895

**Human Resource Development Press**

Publishers of **Human Technology**

Box 863, Dept. M-62, Amherst, Massachusetts 01002
1-413-253-3488

International Standard Book Number: 0-914234-22-6
Library of Congress Number: 77-091639
First Printing — March, 1978

Designed and Illustrated by Tom Capolongo
Consulting Editor, David V. Rowland

2.5

# The Skills of Teaching: Lesson Planning Skills

## TABLE OF CONTENTS

## ABOUT THE AUTHORS

**Dr. Robert R. Carkhuff** is Chairman, Carkhuff Institute of Human Technology. He has devoted his life to research and teaching. The author of more than two dozen books on helping and teaching effectiveness, Dr. Carkhuff is internationally renowned as the most-cited reference in the last decade of counseling psychology. A teacher at primary, secondary and post-secondary levels, he continues to coach youth baseball, basketball and football. Dr. Carkhuff is the developer of the human and educational resources development models upon which **The Skills of Teaching** series is based.

**Sally R. Berenson, M.S. Ed.** is Research Associate in Educational Technology, Carkhuff Institute of Human Technology. She has specialized in curriculum development and has been an elementary and secondary teacher for more than ten years. She has instructed teachers in content development skills at all levels of pre-service and in-service teacher training and is a collaborator on the series, **The Do's and Don'ts of Teaching.**

**Dr. David H. Berenson** is Director of Educational Technology, Carkhuff Institute of Human Technology. He specializes in teacher training and educational administration. A teacher for more than 15 years on elementary and secondary grade levels, Dr. Berenson has spent the last 10 years revolutionizing pre-service and in-service teacher training programs. He has conducted pathfinding research in the development of effective educational delivery systems. Dr. Berenson is co-author of the entire **Skills of Teaching** series.

*The Authors and Their Teachers*

## FOREWORD

In the forefront of the effort to build a human technology are the authors of **The Skills of Teaching** series. With more than a decade of research into teaching and helping processes and outcomes, Dr. Carkhuff and his colleagues have developed the necessary skills teaching programs for a human technology for human effectiveness — skills teaching programs that will enable the children and parents as well as teachers to achieve and enjoy success in learning.

**The Skills of Teaching** represents a landmark in educational technology. These skills programs were developed by and in conjunction with classroom teachers — those in the front lines of education. **The Skills of Teaching** teaches the kind of concrete skills a veteran teacher wishes she had when she began her teaching career. It's the kind of teacher training curriculum that an outstanding teacher-educator might develop over several decades. Human technology is being developed for and by humans.

**The Skills of Teaching** enables teachers to master the teaching skills and, at the same time, to begin to measure the progress of their learners. In time, the learners are able to measure their individual progress and help to control the learning process.

With careful study and planning, teachers and parents soon discover that they are the source of their children's effectiveness. The outcomes are symmetry and harmony. People become truly human beings because they recognize that all of their children are exceptional.

January 1978
Washington, D. C.

James W. Becker, Ed. D.
Executive Director
National Foundation for the
Improvement of Education

In the **National Consortium for Humanizing Education**, we taught **The Skills of Teaching** to hundreds of elementary and secondary teachers all over the country. We studied the effects of our teacher training upon over 6,000 students.

What we found was that learners of teachers with the skills of teaching demonstrated significantly greater growth and development. Most important, teachers could be systematically trained to develop their teaching skills.

Trained teachers were most effective in maintaining **control** and reducing **discipline** problems in the classroom. They were also most effective in facilitating student achievement in **basic skills**.

**The Skills of Teaching** is the most revolutionary step forward in the history of education. Together, the volumes constitute the teacher's answer to accountability: **to preserve the integrity of teaching and produce the accountability of outcome through expanding the quantity and quality of teaching skills.**

We owe a great debt of gratitude to Dr. Carkhuff, Dr. and Mrs. Berenson and their associates for making possible the second greatest privilege in the world — teaching.

January, 1978          David N. Aspy, Ed. D.
Washington, D. C.      Executive Director
                       National Consortium for
                       Humanizing Education

## PREFACE

This volume of **The Skills of Teaching** series focuses upon **Lesson Planning Skills.** These are skills which the teacher uses before and during teaching delivery. Organizing the content, the teacher will have the learners review, overview, present, exercise and summarize. These content organizational skills are combined with the methodological skills of lesson planning.

**Tell** methods describe the content using written or spoken words.

**Show** methods illustrate the content using demonstrations or pictures.

**Do** methods have the learners perform the new learning.

**Repeat** methods have the learners practice the new learning.

**Apply** methods have the students use the new learning in conjunction with previous learnings.

These lesson planning skills will prepare the teacher for the learners. Content development skills, lesson planning skills and interpersonal skills equip the teacher with the basic tools of teacher-effectiveness. They are the teacher's entry into the exciting world of teaching.

January, 1978                                                    D.H.B.
Amherst, Massachusetts                                           S.R.B.
                                                                 R.R.C.

"Class, we have a special new person with us today — Julie Williams." The teacher, Mr. Hanrahan, stood at the front of the room. "Julie's not just another visitor. She's going to be a regular student here in the 4th grade. I hope you'll make her feel right at home."

Julie knew that her new teacher was just trying to be nice. But instead of feeling at home, she felt very nervous. She kept her eyes on her desk, trying to pretend that everyone in the classroom wasn't turning around to look at her. Fortunately for her, Mr. Hanrahan didn't give the other students very much time to stare at the newcomer. In a few moments everyone was looking up at the front of the room again.

"How come you're starting so late?" The blonde girl on Julie's left leaned over and whispered to her.

"My parents just moved here," Julie whispered back, hoping the teacher wouldn't notice her. "I started at another school."

"Oh . . ." Satisfied, the blonde girl turned away again — but not before giving Julie a nice smile that made her feel good. Maybe this girl would be a friend. Julie hoped so because she already missed all of her old friends back at the Tremont School. She sat up straight in her seat and kept her eyes on the teacher, trying to make sure that she didn't miss anything.

"Class, today's lesson is going to be about capitalization," Mr. Hanrahan was saying. Julie watched as he wrote the word on the board:

### CAPITALIZATION

Julie relaxed a little. This shouldn't be too hard. She was good at making capital letters. In fact, her old teacher had told her that she could handle both printing and cursive writing better than almost anyone else in her class!

"Now, who can tell me what kinds of words should start with capital letters?" Mr. Hanrahan asked the class, his eyes sweeping back and forth. Several hands shot up, and he pointed to a chunky boy with glasses and brown hair, sitting in the front row. "O.K., Billy, what kinds of words do you think start with capital letters?"

"Words that start sentences!" Billy announced his answer with a good deal of pride, then folded his arms and looked around at the other kids sitting near him as if to say 'Pretty smart, huh?'

"Great, Billy! You're absolutely right!" Mr. Hanrahan turned back to the board and wrote down this information:

### CAPITALIZATION
All words that start sentences

"But that's not all, is it? Who can think of other kinds of words that always start with capital letters?"

Again, several hands went up. Julie saw that most of the same people seemed to want to answer this second question. And most of the people who had kept their hands down the first time were still not volunteering an answer.

This time Mr. Hanrahan chose a slender black girl in a corner seat of the front row.

"Yes, Marcy. What other kinds of words start with capital letters?"

"Proper nouns start with capital letters," Marcy informed him. Like Billy before her, she couldn't help flashing her neighbors a triumphant grin when Mr. Hanrahan nodded happily and wrote this answer up on the board.

### CAPITALIZATION
All words that start sentences
All proper nouns

"Good, Marcy, you're quite right." He looked around at the class. "I hope the rest of you could have answered these questions as easily as Billy and Marcy did. After all, some of this is stuff you learned last year . . ."

This last comment made Julie nervous all over again. Last year with Ms. Johnson she had learned about capital letters for words that start sentences. But she was sure Ms. Johnson had never said anything about proper nouns. Julie wasn't even sure what a proper noun was! She looked around helplessly, hoping that one of her neighbors might give her a clue. Mr. Hanrahan was moving on though, and everybody's eyes were fixed on him and on the blackboard.

"Now we'll do some group practicing with sentences and proper nouns," he told the class. "Actually, since the sentences are pretty obvious, we'll just concentrate on the nouns."

Once again he turned back to the board. Erasing his earlier notes, he proceeded to write down a number of separate words and phrases.

> jim
> table
> dog
> detroit
> president of the united states
> new york
> judy
> new england
> car
> ford

"Let's start with the first word up here," he said. "As I've written it, the word 'jim' starts with a little 'j.' Is that right or wrong?"

Billy's hand was up at once. "That's wrong," he told Mr. Hanrahan. " 'Jim' is a proper noun, so it should start with a capital 'J.' "

"Right, Billy!" Mr. Hanrahan erased the small 'j' and substituted a capital 'J.' He kept going, moving down the list and never failing to find an eager hand-waver to answer his question. Julie noticed that the same small group of kids kept raising their hands.

The word 'table,' it turned out, was not a proper noun and so did not deserve a capital letter. The same held true for 'dog.' But 'detroit' quickly became 'Detroit.' Mr. Hanrahan approved the capitalization of 'President of the United

States' because, he said, it was the title of someone's job. He also approved the capitalization of 'New York' and the first name 'Judy.'

By now Julie was beginning to feel she understood the pattern behind these mysterious things called proper nouns. So when the next question came, she waved her hand. Mr. Hanrahan spotted this and looked pleased as he called on her.

"Well, Julie, I'm glad to see you getting into things. What's the answer? Should 'new england' be capitalized or not?"

"Yes, it should," Julie told him. The relief she felt when he nodded his head was mixed with a trace of guilt. That had been an easy one — it looked just like 'New York' and he had already said that the latter two words should be capitalized. But it did feel good to be involved in the class.

After they finished the list, Mr. Hanrahan said, "I'd like you to turn to page 34 in your green workbooks and do the exercises on that page. As you'll see, they involve the capitalization of proper nouns. You did so well with our words on the board that I'm sure you'll have no trouble at all!"

Julie obediently took her new green workbook out of her desk and turned to page 34. Here she found a list of sentences. As Mr. Hanrahan had promised, the instructions told her to go over each sentence and capitalize all proper nouns.

"I'm glad I'm getting to start with something easy," she whispered to her blonde neighbor.

The other girl gave her a funny look. "If you think this is easy, you must be a brain or something!" Then she bent over her work. Somewhat surprised, Julie did the same. But it **was** easy! The first sentence even included some of the same words Mr. Hanrahan had put on the board.

1. "As a truck driver, tom smith drove all over new york and new england and saw many exciting new places."

"This is really simple," Julie said to herself. She capitalized 'truck driver' because it named the man's job. She capitalized 'tom' because it was a name just like 'jim' or 'judy.' Then she capitalized 'new york,' 'new england' and 'new places' because they all started with the same word, 'new' — an obvious tip-off! Her revised sentence looked like this:

1. As a Truck Driver, Tom smith drove all over New York and New England and saw many exciting New Places."

The other sentences, Julie was pleased to see, were equally simple. She was able to finish the paper well before the bell rang. With the rest of the class, she filed past Mr. Hanrahan's desk and put her completed worksheet on the pile.

The blonde girl was waiting for her in the hall. "My name's Linda," she told Julie. "Boy, you must be really smart to know all that stuff already."

Julie grinned at her. It was nice to meet someone so friendly on her very first day at her new school. She didn't want to spoil things by sounding too proud of herself. But she couldn't keep just a trace of pleasure from her voice.

"Well, I didn't really know it already," she confided in Linda as they moved down the hall. "Not exactly. We didn't study proper nouns last year in my old school so I had to figure it out for myself." Thinking this sounded a little snooty she added: "I guess the kids at this school learned more than I did last year."

But Linda just laughed. "No we didn't! Mr. Hanrahan thought everyone knew about proper nouns — but the only kids who did were the ones up in front who were in Mr. Amico's class last year. The rest of us just played along. Mr. Hanrahan gets all confused if we start telling him what we don't know. It's better this way."

This surprised Julie. Once again she was glad the exercises had been so simple. Then she forgot the class and concentrated on her new friend.

"We're s'posed to go to lunch now, aren't we? But I don't even know where that is."

Linda laughed. "C'mon, I'll show you!" And she raced down the hall with Julie in tow.

It was going to be O.K. at her new school, Julie thought as she ran. After all, look how much she'd learned already!

## CHAPTER 1: INTRODUCTION

**Teaching: The Second Greatest Privilege**

This is the second most important moment of your life, You stand in front of your own class for the first time.

Many of you have yet to experience that moment. You may still be preparing for your first student teaching experience. Yet many more remember the moment well.

It is the day you fully become an adult, taking responsibility for the lives of others. The rites of student teaching mark your passage from the first to the second greatest privilege in the world: from learner to teacher. It is a scary moment. You stand alone in front of the class. The helpful people who taught you are with you only in knowledge and spirit. It is your moment. You think "If only my supervisor won't stay too long."

If you have teaching skills, you are ready to teach.

Teaching a lesson in front of a supervisor or principal can be an unsettling experience for you as a new teacher. You will never be quite as nervous again. Perhaps your hands shake a little and turn ice cold. Or your stomach works overtime. Whatever your nervous symptoms are, you want your evaluation to be a good one.

In front of your class, you may glance once more in desperation at your lesson plan. You feel like a swimmer going down for the third time.

"I hope the kids will be good!" You worry, "What if the projector breaks!" You consider everything that could go wrong.

Then it is time to begin. You focus on your learners and what you have planned to teach. In a very short time you will be teaching. Hopefully, the students will be learning. And, if you are teaching effectively, you will forget who is sitting in the back of the room . . . almost!

## Planning the Content

Before the supervisor's visit, you turn your attention to the content of the lesson you will teach. You organize the class time according to your lesson plan form. First, you write the content of the review or introduction. Next, you plan the content of your procedure or presentation. The last part of your lesson may include some practice or assignment for the learners. In any case, you will want to vary what you will teach during the class time. You want to make sure that your content will receive a good evaluation.

If you vary your teaching, your lessons will be more dynamic.

### Planning the Methods

In planning how you will teach, you consider various methods. You could use questions and answers to start the class — or maybe a game. You want the supervisor to be interested early in the lesson.

You may think, "Questions are too dull. We'll play a game to introduce the lesson. The kids will like that, too."

After deciding what other methods you will use to teach, you feel more confident. Perhaps you have selected a panel discussion, poster-making or a laboratory experience for your learners. You want your learners to be involved and your methods to be varied. This is another way to impress the supervisor with your teaching ability.

If you have lesson planning skills, then you will teach with direction.

You may never really be sure if you have included everything you need to make your teaching delivery as good as it can be. Your education courses have given you some general principles to work from. Change bulletin boards frequently. Vary methods of activities. Be alive and dynamic. Dress neatly and appropriately.

But all of this advice has not told you how to teach. You still ask, "But how . . .?"

**The Skills of Teaching – Lesson Planning Skills** provides a detailed outline of the specific skills you will need to plan and deliver each day's content. You already know a great deal about your materials — the content you want to teach. Now you must be able to develop the best possible **lesson plans** to ensure that your students learn what you teach them each day. For in the end, they are your most important critics. Not your supervisor. Not your principal. But the roomful of learners who watch and listen and work and play in your classroom every day! It is their educational growth and behavior that tell you how effective you are as a teacher. Stated simply, you cannot be effective without good lesson planning skills.

Teaching a lesson is as complex for teachers as it is critical to the learners. It is the process that transmits what the teacher knows to the learners. Some teachers' lessons are very effective. Their students are truly learners. Over the year these learners acquire many new skills from their teacher. And not just a few learners. The teacher reaches everyone in the class. What do these teachers do that makes the difference? First, you may want to look at their interpersonal relationships with the learners (see **Skills of Teaching — Interpersonal Skills**). You will probably find that these teachers interact with all the learners very skillfully. Next, examine the content that these teachers deliver (see **Skills of Teaching — Content Development Skills**). The content will relate closely with the learners' needs and abilities. Then study the teachers' **lessons**. These teachers will integrate their content with a variety of teaching methods and thus communicate the content to their learners most effectively.

If you have interpersonal skills and content development skills, you will be able to communicate your lesson plan.

## PRE-TRAINING LESSON PLANNING OVERVIEW

### Learning to Explore, Understand and Act

There are three phases of learning. The first phase is **exploring** the new learning. As you read this material, you are exploring where you are in relation to lesson planning skills. Taking into consideration what you already know about lesson planning, you are exploring what else you need to learn. Having determined what you know, the next phase is **understanding** what you need to know. When you explore the skills of lesson planning, you will understand more fully the function of the new skills. You understand how the new pieces fit with the old pieces so that you are ready for the third phase of learning: **acting**. When you **explore** what you know and **understand** what you need to know, then you can **act** to write a lesson plan.

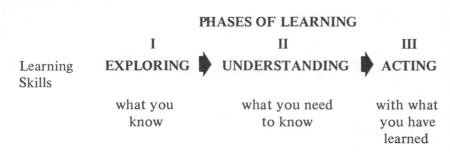

**PHASES OF LEARNING**

|  | I | | II | | III |
|---|---|---|---|---|---|
| Learning Skills | **EXPLORING** | ▶ | **UNDERSTANDING** | ▶ | **ACTING** |
|  | what you know | | what you need to know | | with what you have learned |

## 10 Helping the Learners to Explore, Understand and Act

The learners can be taught effectively when you help them **explore** the new learning first. You can give them an opportunity to explore what they know and what they do not know about the new learning. As your learners explore, you may hear them say:

"What's this called?"
"What does this do?"
"Is this right?"

In the second phase, you can help your learners **understand** what they do not know. The more the learners understand, the more often you will hear them say:

"This goes here!"
"I see how this works now!"
"I think I can do it!"

Finally, you will help the learners to **act** in the last phase of learning. Then they will begin to say:

"I can do that!"
"It's my turn!"
"Look at mine!"

Helping your learners to **explore, understand** and **act** will maximize your success in teaching and your learners' success with learning.

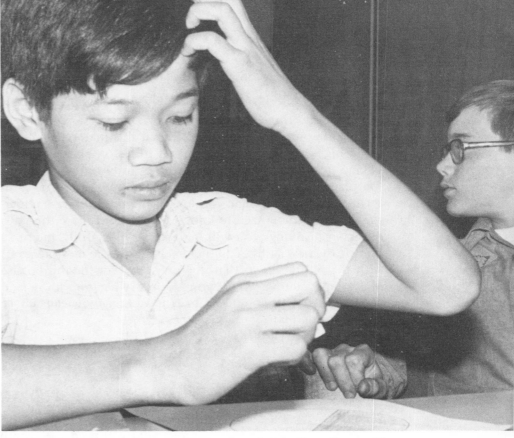

If your students explore, understand and act, then they will learn what you teach.

# HELPING THE LEARNERS WITH INTERPERSONAL SKILLS

### Attending

Interpersonal skills are the delivery skills of teaching. Bridging the gap between the content and the learners, they make the difference between those teachers who relate the content effectively, and those who do not. Consider **attending,** the first set of interpersonal skills. You use attending skills with the learners before they begin to explore. Attending to the learners, you circulate around the room, positioning yourself to pay attention to them. You make eye contact with the group of learners. Most importantly, when you speak with them you approach and face them squarely, observing and listening fully to them.

**PHASES OF LEARNING**

| | | I | II | III |
|---|---|---|---|---|
| Teacher: | Interpersonal Skills | Attending | | |
| Learner: | Learning Skills | Exploring what you know | Understanding what you need to know | Acting to learn what you need to know |

There are many ways to attend to your learners. Positioning yourself in relation to the students communicates your interest in them. Attending prepares you to receive information about the students by just watching and listening to what is happening in the classroom. Communicating interest and receiving input, you are equipped to involve the learners in the learning experience. When using attending skills, you will find yourself saying:

"Rachel is staring out the window again! Maybe she needs some help."

"Whatever is Kenneth doing wandering around the room? Does he have all of his materials?"

"Jason is finished. I'll get him started on the reading."

When you attend to your learners, you will help them prepare for learning.

## Responding

Not only will you attend to the learners, but you will also **respond**. When you use responding skills in your delivery, you help the learners to explore. Responding skills help you enter the learners' frame of reference. You begin to get an idea of where they are "coming from." These skills reveal to you and the learners what they know and do not know. If all learning begins with the learners' frames of reference, then it is only appropriate to employ responding skills to enter those frames of reference. The effective teacher shies away from the sermonizing "It's your own fault you haven't learned your number facts," and responds to the learners — "You get frustrated because you have to count on your fingers." This second response communicates a real understanding of the learners and their experience. Then the learners may be motivated to learn the number facts; not because you have told them to, but because you understand their experience of where they are in relation to their learning tasks when they do not have to count on their fingers anymore.

## PHASES OF LEARNING

| Teacher: | Interpersonal Skills | Attending ▶ Responding |
| Learner: | Learning Skills | ⬇ Exploring |

Attending skills prepare you to respond to the learners. Responding skills help your learners to explore what they do and do not know. As your learners attack new skills, you will respond to their feelings and the reasons for their feelings. You might say "You all feel pretty good about doing this experiment, but you aren't quite sure how to write it up." Then you may hear the learners explore the task when they say:

"Experiments are fun to do, but the reports are hard."

"What do you write down first?"

"I never know where to begin!"

Then the learners are ready for more of your teaching skills.

When you respond to your learners, you will help the learners explore the new learning.

**Personalizing**

In addition to attending and responding, you need **personalizing** skills. When you personalize for your learners, they understand more fully what they need to learn. Your responding skills have let you enter your learners' frames of reference so that you can personalize the new learning for the learners. You not only see the learning situation through your learners' eyes, but can also relate their experiences to the learning task. You personalize the learners' experiences of the lesson so that they will understand their individual learning goals.

## PHASES OF LEARNING

| | | | | |
|---|---|---|---|---|
| Teacher: | Interpersonal Skills | Attending ▶ | Responding | Personalizing |
| Learner: | Learning Skills | | Exploring | Understanding |

Having responded to the learners in the exploration phase of learning, you will move toward personalizing in the understanding phase of learning. You may say, "You feel mixed-up because you don't know when to start a new sentence." Then your learners will understand what they need to know, and may respond to you as they begin to understand:

"I just don't know where to put the period!"

"It seems okay to me, but then you mark it wrong!"

"How are you supposed to do it?"

When you personalize, your learners can understand what they need to learn.

## Initiating

In the last phase of teaching delivery, you will use **initiating** skills. You facilitate the learners' ability to act so that they may learn what they need to know. To do that, you systematically break down the learning into steps. These are steps that your learners can manage — not too large, not too small. You develop programs that include the learners' goals: "Your goal is to begin learning the '2' number facts." You develop programs that include a first step that comes from the learners' frames of reference: "Your first step is to write down the hypothesis or what you were trying to prove in the experiment." You develop the remaining steps to reach the learning goal: "These are the five steps you should take in writing a good, complete sentence."

### PHASES OF LEARNING

| | | I | II | III |
|---|---|---|---|---|
| Teacher: | Interpersonal Skills | | | |
| | | Attending ▶ Responding | Personalizing | Initiating |
| Learner: | Learning Skills | Exploring | Understanding | Acting |

## 18  Initiating Improves Learners' Action

With increased initiating skills, the quality of your learners' action will improve considerably. When the learners act, they recycle the phases of learning, using the feedback they get: they explore the relationships between the different parts of what they are doing; they understand a new concept of how these parts fit together; they prepare to act again to test new ideas. When you initiate with appropriate programs that come from your learners' frames of reference, you ensure their success in the action phase of learning. As they act, you may hear them say:

"So that's why the wheel goes around!"

"I wonder what would happen if I put some oil on the axle?"

"See! We did it!"

When you initiate, your learners can act with the learning.

**Developing Content**

Organizing what and how you will teach requires another set of skills. You need planning skills to teach effectively. Just as you attend to the learners before they begin to explore, you will **develop a content** before you begin planning the delivery. You will decide what content your learners need to explore. Breaking down that content into sets of skills is the first step of content development. Then you develop the steps required to perform the skills. In addition, you will examine the supportive knowledge that the learners may need to perform the skills successfully.

## PHASES OF TEACHING AND LEARNING

| Teacher: | Teacher Preparing Skills | Developing Content |
|---|---|---|
| Learner: | Learning Skills | |

Whether your content is in the form of a prescribed curriculum or a textbook series, you will evaluate that content, modifying it to fit the needs of your learners. You may say to yourself, "My learners need to learn some spelling skills. I'll start with adding suffixes to one syllable words." Then you may consider just one of these skills: "adding 'ing' to a word with a long vowel and silent 'e' will be the first skill. The steps are: 1) consonant-vowel-consonant-'e' word; 2) drop silent 'e'; 3) add 'ing'." Finally you will determine what supportive knowledge the learners may need: "I'll want to make sure the learners know the long vowel sounds!" Developing your content in this manner leads you to the next phase of teaching preparation: diagnosis.

If you develop your content, you have defined your teaching goals.

## Diagnosing

Whereas your content is a pre-condition of preparation, **diagnostic** skills are those that you will use to facilitate the exploration phase of learning. You will prepare your diagnosis of the learners in relation to the content you choose to teach. You will use your diagnostic skills to help your learners explore where they are in relation to the learning experience. Diagnosing the learners with respect to the content tells you and the learners what they know and do not know.

### PHASES OF TEACHING AND LEARNING

I

Teacher:    Teaching    Developing ▶ Diagnosing
Preparation  Content
Skills

Learner:    Learning              Exploring
Skills

To diagnose your learners in relation to the content, you will determine if they have already mastered the set of skills. You plan a diagnosis that will tell you and the learners how well they can use the skills. The diagnosis can also tell you what parts of the skills they can and cannot use. You will plan to diagnose the supportive knowledge of the skills also. An oral or written diagnosis can be planned for this exploratory phase of learning. When you diagnose, you may hear the learners say:

"I can spell these words, but I got those wrong."

"I really need help with my spelling!"

"Will you teach us how to do this stuff?"

When you diagnose your learners, you explore where they are in relation to your content.

**Setting Goals**

Once you have implemented your diagnosis, you use the results to **set goals** for the learners. In the understanding phase of learning, you help the learners understand what needs to be learned and why. The results of this diagnosis are used to give direction to the learning process. You need to prepare these goals in relation to the content. If your content does not include skills that the learners need, then you add the missing contents and their parts. You use your goal-setting skills to help your learners understand where they are in relation to where they need to be in the learning experience.

**PHASES OF TEACHING AND LEARNING**

| | | | I | II |
|---|---|---|---|---|
| Teacher: | Teaching Preparation Skills | Developing Content | ▶ Diagnosing | Setting Goals |
| Learner: | Learning Skills | | Exploring | Understanding |

When you set appropriate goals for the learners, you are helping them to understand. Going back into the content, you select the skills and knowledge your learners need to understand. You are preparing for goal-setting when you say: "The learners need to practice short vowel sounds." Then you go back to your content to write a program that the learners can use to learn the short vowel sounds. Next, using the diagnosis, you will set goals for the learners so that they can understand.

"I can spell words with long vowels, but I got the words with short 'i' and 'e' wrong."
"I can't tell the difference between the way they sound."
"Can you help me?"

When you set goals for your learners, you define the content of your lesson plans.

In the last phase of preparation, you will write **lesson plans** in order to deliver the content. Having diagnosed and set goals for the learners in relation to a content, you will plan the methods to use to deliver that content. In planning your lesson, you prepare for the delivery or the acting phase of learning. The learners can then act to learn what they need to learn. They can act to get from where they are to where they want to be in relation to the learning experience. When you plan the lesson, you will use a variety of methods to teach the content. You will also plan exercises which have the learners repeat and apply the content. Planning your diagnosis, goal-setting and lesson planning begins from your learners' frames of reference and is implemented by your preparation and interpersonal skills.

## PHASES OF TEACHING AND LEARNING

|  |  |  | I | II | III |
|---|---|---|---|---|---|
| Teacher: | Teaching Preparation Skills | Developing Content | ▶ Diagnosing | Setting Goals | Planning Lessons |
| Learner: | Learning Skills |  | Exploring | Understanding | Acting |

The initiating phase of teaching delivery requires the preparation of a lesson plan based on the goals, thus maximizing the learning experience for the students. The lesson plan should present the content you plan to teach and the methods you plan to use. You may want to use a tape recorder in order to have the learners hear the short vowel sounds. You may want to use an overhead projector to show the learners how to identify short vowel patterns. You may want to have the learners use a worksheet to do the skill. The learners can practice repeating the skill in teams of two: one speaking, the other spelling. Finally, the learners could apply the skills by spelling the words in a game. And as your learners act, you may hear them say:

"I think I can do it now!"

"This is easy!"

When you diagnose and set goals for your learners, then you are ready to plan your lesson.

You need effective skills that will enable you to write a lesson plan — these are the skills you will learn as you progress through this book. First, you will learn how to organize the content you will teach. You will organize the content you will **review** and the content you will **overview**. Next, you will consider the content of the **presentation, exercise** and **summary**. The acronym you can use to remember this content organization is **ROPES**.

After you have prepared the content, you will examine it in respect to the methods you will use to deliver that content. You have been told what methods **not** to use with much more frequency than you have been told what **to** use. "Don't talk all the time." "Get the kids involved in the learning!" Have you ever stopped to ask why this should be true? It is not only because it is boring to use the same method of communicating; it is because not all learners are auditory. While some learners learn with their ears, others learn with their eyes. So when you teach, you not only **tell** the students about the learning, you **show** them too. But even telling and showing are not enough to have the learners master what you are teaching. You must plan to have the students **do** the learning. They will then have an opportunity to see, hear and manipulate what you want them to learn. As simple as it sounds, content and methods are what lesson planning is all about — matching up your content with appropriate methods.

### Using Lesson Planning Skills

You may never have written a lesson plan before; or you may have written hundreds of lesson plans. Regardless of your experience, you will want to measure your lesson planning skill level before you begin this training experience. This assessment will enable you to explore more fully the skills you have and the skills you do not have. We will ask you to write a lesson plan in your specialty area. Begin by selecting a **skill** you would teach your learners. This skill should be something that you want your learners to be able to do. You may want them to be able to write a complete sentence, state the story problem, sequence events, draw a number line, convert meters to centimeters, categorize objects or saw a piece of wood. Describe what you would teach and how you would teach that skill.

Skill: _____

You may feel unsure at this point about your ability to write a complete lesson plan. The discrimination task may be more comfortable for you to do. Somehow, it seems easier to distinguish a good lesson plan from a poor one than to write a good one yourself. We will ask you to rate five lesson plans. Some are more complete than others. Use a five-point scale to rate these plans where the least complete plan is rated 1.0 and the most complete plan is rated 5.0.

1.0   Very Ineffective

2.0   Ineffective

3.0   Minimally Effective

4.0   Very Effective

5.0   Extremely Effective

If you feel a lesson falls between two levels on the scale, you may rate it as 1.5, 2.5, 3.5 or 4.5. For example, suppose the lesson plan seemed better than "minimally effective," but not quite "very effective." You would rate that plan 3.5. You may use a rating more than once.

1. Teacher tells the class that the review skill is finding the main idea of the reading.
2. Teacher shows the first transparency which tells the first step of the skill: a) Read chapter once. Show overlay with an example from previous class. Learners read the chapter in the text.
3. Teacher continues as in step 2 with the remaining steps: b) Ask, "What is this chapter about?" c) Read the subtitles; d) Turn subtitles into a 'what' question; e) Find main idea.
4. Teacher conducts an experiment with class. First, the learners try to take down everything the teaacher says while reading a paragraph.
5. Then students listen to another paragraph the teacher reads and write down the gist of what was said when the teacher finishes.
6. Teacher discusses results with the students to show the need for an efficient system to record knowledge that will be needed at a later date. That system is called **outlining**.
7. Teacher tells the steps involved in writing an outline and writes them on the chalkboard: a) Title; b) Roman Numerals; c) Capital Letters; d) Numbers; e) Lower-Case Letters.
8. Teacher shows sample outline on overhead which describes how to write an outline.
9. Students take turns reading the outlined steps and then telling how they would do each step from their own reading of the chapter in the science textbook.
10. Students write their own outlines completely from the reading.
11. Teacher reviews the steps of writing an outline with the transparency that was previously used.
12. Students give examples from their own outline of each step.

**Lesson Plan B: Brushing Your Teeth**      **Your Rating:** _____

1. In order to review the skill of holding and moving a toothbrush, the teacher asks a learner to stand up in front of the class and show the other learners how to hold a toothbrush.
2. Teacher places magnetized placards of each step in random order on the chalkboard. Teacher asks learners to write the order they would pick to do the skill.
3. Learners take turns putting placards in order: a) Use hand you write with; b) Place the brush between your thumb and index finger so that the end of the handle is in your palm; c) Slide thumb up handle toward bristles; d) Hold handle with other fingers; e) Move brush up and down.
4. Teacher shows some slides of different children's teeth, illustrating various degrees of care.
5. Teacher asks different students what they think about the slides.
6. Teacher tells the learners about tooth and gum diseases illustrated by slides and how these conditions relate to tooth brushing.
7. Teacher shows the learners how to follow these steps using a large model of teeth and a giant tooth brush.
8. The steps are: a) Wet the brush and apply the toothpaste; b) Brush all surfaces of the upper teeth; c) Brush all surfaces of the lower teeth.
9. Learners write down the steps of tooth brushing in their notebooks.
10. Learners review the steps by making an audio tape which describes the steps in their own words.
11. Learners make posters for Dental Week which illustrate good mouth hygiene practices.

1. Teacher places, on a flip chart in front of the class, a model U.S. map that is divided into four quarters.
2. Teacher points out the major points of outlining the first quarter. Teacher tells the learners the following: a) Divide the paper into quarters with ruler and faint pencil lines; b) Start lightly in upper right hand quarter; c) Use model on flip chart; d) Look at model; e) Sketch lightly; f) Look at sketch; g) Repeat until first quarter looks like model; h) Make a second quarter, fourth quarter, then third quarter; i) Redraw map over light sketch lines.
3. Teacher places these steps on the chalkboard for the learners.
4. Teacher overviews the reasons for people wanting to settle in the west.
5. Students vote to see if they would have liked to take the risks on leaving their homes to travel in new lands.
6. Teacher tallies the vote on the chalkboard to be used later in the class.
7. Teacher tells the students about the journeys that were made westward. Vivid descriptions are read to the students from the diary of a young pioneer girl.
8. Learners make a list of what they would have to leave behind them if they were going to leave their homes to live in the wilderness.
9. Teacher describes the various routes the pioneers took and then asks the learners to list what they would have to take with them if they were going the northern route or the southern route.
10. Teacher reviews lesson by having the learners write a sentence telling how they would feel about leaving their home. She puts these on the bulletin board.

**Lesson Plan D: Adding 'ing' to Words**     **Your Rating:** _____

1. Teacher asks several learners how to read "pip" and "pipe." The teacher asks how they knew the vowel was short, how they knew the vowel was long.
2. The learners write out the steps of CVC: a) If CVC pattern, b) The vowel is short, c) i = in, a = apple, e = egg, o = on, u = up. a) If CVCE pattern, b) Vowel is long, c) a = ape, e = eat, i = ice, o = oat, u = use.
3. Learners put a list of long and short vowels into two lists, the first short vowels, the second for long vowels. Teacher gives immediate feedback.
4. Teacher gives a spelling test of five words ending in **ing**: busing, eating, swimming, boning, sunning.
5. Students exchange papers to correct spelling, giving numerical grades based on 100%.
6. Teacher explains that once the students learn how to add **ing** to a word, they will be able to spell more accurately. Then she reads the spelling words for the learners and writes them on the board for them to see.
7. Teacher puts "dot" and "dote" on an overhead transparency. One learner reads the words and two others define the words. Two learners put a sentence on the chalkboard that uses these words.
8. Teacher shows an overlay of the steps to take to add "ing" to these words. Then he shows them how to change "cane" to "caning" and "can" to "canning."
9. The learners all add "ing" to "dot" and "dote."
10. The teacher circulates around the room while the learners do a worksheet, adding "ing" to long and short vowel words.
11. Students summarize what they have learned by writing the steps in their notebooks, using the words in the spelling test as an example.

1. Teacher has learners write down favorite number between 0 and 100. Teacher makes a list on chalkboard. Teacher selects all numbers less than ten and asks "What are they called?" (Answer: ones.) Teacher writes down the first two steps of naming numbers on chalkboard. a) One's place is first place on right; b) Name of ones, 0 - 9.

2. Teacher repeats the above directions with the tens. She writes down the next two steps: a) Ten's place is second place from right; b) Names of tens, 10, 20 . . . 90. For a number with tens and ones, the teacher writes down the last step; c) For 21 - 99, name the ten's number, then the one's number. Learners take turns reading their numbers from the board while teacher points to ten's and one's place. Teacher explains 11 - 19 names.

3. Learners follow steps on chalkboard to write the names of the following: 35, 48, 64, 93, 29.

4. Teacher passes back a test on subtraction where the majority of mistakes were made with the regrouping process. The learners try to correct their errors. Teacher circulates around the room helping them individually.

5. Teacher uses a common error to point out to the learners their lack of skill in regrouping.

6. After the learners have finished correcting their errors, the teacher puts the following steps on a flip-chart: a) Start with one's column. Do you need to regroup? b) If no, subtract ones, c) If yes, regroup a ten from ten's column. d) Subtract ones. e) Subtract tens.

7. Learners take turns reading the steps while teacher performs the subtraction of a sample problem. First with blocks and then on the board.

8. Groups of six learners come to the board to complete an example until everyone has had a turn.

9. Learners do worksheet of ten examples. When they finish, they form committees of 4.

10. Groups circulate around room solving simulated grocery store problems.

11. Teacher reviews steps while correcting these problems with the class and then gives class one more example in which regrouping is used.

## 36  Checking Out Your Lesson Planning Discrimination:

You may be eager to see how well you did in rating the teacher's lesson plans. We will give you feedback on your ability to discriminate effective from ineffective lesson plans.

Trained raters, who have demonstrated the validity of their ratings in studies of teaching, rated each of the preceding lesson plans on their level of completeness. These ratings are listed in the table below. After comparing your ratings with those below you may wish to determine your discrimination score.

| Lesson Plan | Rating |
|---|---|
| A.  Outlining | 3.0 |
| B.  Brushing Teeth | 2.0 |
| C.  Mapping | 1.0 |
| D.  Adding "ing" | 4.0 |
| E.  Regrouping | 5.0 |

## Obtaining Your Discrimination Score

Use the table of ratings to determine your discrimination as follows:

1. Regardless of whether the difference is positive or negative, write down the difference between each of your numerical ratings and each of the trained raters' numerical ratings.
2. Add up the difference scores for each rating. You should have 5 difference scores since there were 5 lesson plans.
3. Divide the total of the difference scores by the total number of ratings, 5. The resulting number is your discrimination score.

Follow the example below which shows how a score is determined from a hypothetical set of ratings.

### EXAMPLE

| Lesson Plan | Ratings | | Hypothetical Ratings | | Difference (Deviation from Raters) | |
|---|---|---|---|---|---|---|
| A: Outlining | 3.0 | – | 5.0 | = | 2 | |
| B: Brushing Teeth | 2.0 | – | 3.0 | = | 1 | |
| C: Mapping | 1.0 | – | 3.0 | = | 2 | Step 1) Subtract |
| D: Adding "ing" | 4.0 | – | 2.0 | = | 2 | |
| E: Regrouping | 5.0 | – | 4.0 | = | 1 | |
| | | | Total | = | 8 | Step 2) Total |
| | | | | | 5 | Step 3) Divide |
| | | | Lesson Plan Discrimination Score | = | 1.6 | |

| Lesson Plan | Ratings | | Your Ratings | | Difference (Deviation from Raters) | |
|---|---|---|---|---|---|---|
| A: Outlining | 3.0 | – | _____ | = | _____ | |
| B: Brushing Teeth | 2.0 | – | _____ | = | _____ | Step 1) Subtract |
| C: Mapping | 1.0 | – | _____ | = | _____ | |
| D: Adding "ing" | 4.0 | – | _____ | = | _____ | |
| E: Regrouping | 5.0 | – | _____ | = | _____ | |
| | | | Total | = | _____ | Step 2) Total |
| | | | | | 5 | Step 3) Divide |
| | | | Pre-Training Lesson Planning = Discrimination Score | | _____ | |

You may be interested in knowing more about the ratings of the lesson plans so that you can understand more about what you will be learning in this text. The outlining lesson plan (A) was rated as "minimally effective" at 3.0. This plan provided for **telling** the learners how to outline as well as **showing** them how to do the new skill. The learners were to **do** the skill as well. The mapping lesson (C) at first glance seemed very good but was rated 1.0 or "very ineffective." On closer look, you will find that it never teaches the students how to map the western routes. There are no skill steps except in the review and then the teacher only **tells** the learners how to sketch a map. The tooth brushing lesson (B) told the learners how to brush their teeth and showed them the skill steps. However, it was rated ineffective, or 2.0, because it did not provide the learners with an opportunity to **do** the skill. Writing the steps is not **doing** the steps. The remaining plans (D and E) were rated above 3.0 because they not only included the elements of the outlining plan but also a student exercise. There were provisions made for the learners to **repeat** the skill in each plan. The regrouping lesson plan (E) rated highest (5.0) because it planned to have the learners **apply** the skill as well as **repeat** it.

## Understanding the Reason for the Rating

You have received a measure of your skill in terms of rating lesson plans. If your discrimination score was greater than .5 and thus your ratings deviated more than one-half level on the average, your discrimination skills are not as accurate as you will want them. Then **your** goal will be to learn to effectively discriminate lesson plans.

Look back to the lesson plan you wrote.

1. Did you plan to **tell** and **show** the learners how to do the skill steps?
2. Did you include the **skill steps** in your plan?
3. Did you plan to have the learners **do** the actual skill?

If you answered "no" to any one question, then your level of writing lesson plans is less than effective. In that case, your goal will be to learn to write effective lesson plans.

### The Teaching Ingredients

You have had your first taste of programmatic feedback on your teaching preparation skills. Those of you with teaching experience may have found it helpful to learn ways to further define what you have found to be the ingredients of effective teaching. Yes, these are models for effective teaching. Most importantly, they are skills that you can test out in your daily experience. You learn to trust the feedback from your learners. If the skills are useful, they will help to make your teaching more effective. These are simple lessons for the student teacher. They were paid for by the intensity of the teaching and learning efforts of experienced teachers. Feedback has helped to shape their teaching effectiveness and the experienced teachers remember well how this learning came about.

If you increase your teaching skills, you will increase your teaching effectiveness.

Martha hurried across the campus toward Dana Hall. The long shadows of late summer spread over the early morning grass. And even though it was still summer, the air had a fresh, autumn sparkle. "I really can't be late," Martha mumbled as she ran up the steps. "Especially not today!"

It was an important morning for Martha. Along with the other members of her education class, she would receive her student teaching assignment and meet with her supervisor. She was getting ready to do her student teaching.

Inside, a group of students were clustered around the bulletin board announcing student teaching assignments.

"Adams School! ALL RIGHT!" Peggy Burns squealed as she elbowed her way out of the crowd.

"Not North School! That school should be closed down!" George Jackson grumbled, looking disappointed.

"Hey! Let me see," pleaded Martha. "C'mom you guys." Martha worked her way up to the front of the group. "Oh, no! Not the Campus School! I'll never make it!"

"Peggy, you have all the luck," said Martha as the two girls walked down the hall to the seminar room.

"Oh, c'mon, Martha! No sour grapes, huh? We're finally going to get a chance to teach. And that's exciting!"

"Yeah! But you got the best school, Peggy. You know I'm never going to be able to please those teachers at the Campus School. They think they've got all the answers!"

Peggy smiled. "Well! They have had **some** experience, Martha. Who knows? Maybe you'll even learn something for a change."

". . . and in addition, you will keep a complete set of lesson plans which will be graded at the end of each week of student teaching."

Martha looked up at Dr. Bollas with a good deal of apprehension. "On top of everything else, he wants lesson plans, too! I'll never make it," she told herself. Around her, the other students reacted with varying degrees of concern.

"Dr. Bollas! We've never written lesson plans before. We don't even know where to begin," said George.

"I've heard a lot of talk about lesson plans, but I've never seen one," joined in Peggy. "What do you include? How long should they . . ."

"Hold on, interrupted Dr. Bollas. "You're telling me that you feel concerned because you've never written lesson plans before!"

"That's right!"

"You better believe it!"

"Right on!"

"You're really upset because you don't even know where to begin," he responded as the students nodded their heads. "Then let's start by learning how to write a lesson plan. That's what these seminars are all about — helping you with your student teaching."

"The first thing you have to do is decide what you are going to teach. That's your content. We'll spend the rest of this seminar learning how to organize that content."

Peggy looked over at Martha and raised her eyebrows. "See! We ARE going to learn something," she whispered. Martha smiled but still looked skeptical. "I'll believe it when I see it!"

## CHAPTER 2: ORGANIZING YOUR CONTENT: REVIEW-OVERVIEW-PRESENTATION-EXERCISE-SUMMARY

### Experiencing Organizing Content

Before each week begins, you plan daily lessons for that week. Using your textbooks and curriculum, you write out the content of the lesson plans. This helps you think through what content you will teach. You need to know **what** you will teach before you can decide **how** to teach it. Some experienced teachers may contend that they no longer need to write lesson plans. In most cases however, they do not teach a skill-based curriculum or do not use a variety of teaching methods. You may even suspect that they are not as effective as they could be. An outstanding teacher will work to make each class more effective than the last. Not happy with last year's success, that teacher will find new and better ways of teaching. Good teachers want to grow as much as their learners . . . and to do that, both have to work.

Learners help their teachers to grow.

Before you can complete a lesson plan, you need to answer the questions "What is it that I am going to teach?" and "How am I going to teach it?"

Throughout this book, we will emphasize the teaching of skills to your learners. You want your learners to be able to **do** something when they finish the year with you. It is not enough for them to "know" things. They need to be able to act upon what they know. That is how you will know if you have done your job. Your effectiveness can be measured by the skills your learners have acquired. Even in your own case, it would not be enough for you to "know" things about teaching. Being able to define "standard deviation" or "understand the phonetic rules of reading" is not sufficient to make you a good teacher. You need to learn the **skills** of teaching. First, you need to learn to organize your content in order to be able to deliver your skills to your learners. You must learn to organize your content before you can prepare your lesson plans.

## PRE-TRAINING ASSESSMENT OF CONTENT ORGANIZATION SKILLS

### Using Organizing Skills

You have some idea of the content you will teach your learners. This assumes that you have thought about your learners to determine what content they need to learn.

Writing down the content you will teach is really the beginning of your lesson plan. Take the time now to write what you would teach your learners about a skill they need to learn. Write an **outline of the skill content** as you would teach it. In this way, you can get an index of your level of content organizing skills.

Make sure that you select a **skill** to teach your learners. Very simply, a skill is something you want your learners to be able to do. Do not select a topic which simply has your learners use recall to make a list or define words. You will want to select a skill which has your learners do something that you can see and measure — something that they can repeat. Drawing a cube, finding the predicate, mixing the color green and dividing a three-digit number by a one-digit number are examples of skills that your learners may need to learn.

# CONTENT OUTLINE

Skill: _____

You may be concerned that your lesson's content is not complete. Perhaps it was difficult to write down exactly what you would teach. The next task will probably be easier for you. We are going to ask you to rate the content of five teachers' lessons. Some are more complete than others. To test your ability to discriminate the organization of the content of a lesson, rate them on a scale from 1.0 to 5.0 in which 1.0 is the least complete organization and 5.0 is the most complete organization.

1.0   Very Ineffective

2.0   Ineffective

3.0   Minimally Effective

4.0   Very Effective

5.0   Extremely Effective

If you feel a lesson falls between two levels on the scale, you may rate it as 1.5, 2.5, 3.5 or 4.5. For example, suppose the lesson plan seemed somewhere between "ineffective" and "minimally effective." You would give that lesson plan a rating of 2.5. You may use a rating more than once.

Remember that you are rating only **what** these teachers are planning to teach, not **how** they are planning to teach. Later we will deal with teaching methods.

Teacher A wanted her students to learn how to outline a chapter in their science textbooks. Before the learners did the outline, Teacher A wanted to make sure they were ready for the new skill. Sitting at her desk, she thought about what the learners needed to know before they tried the outline. She decided that they could use a review of reading to pinpoint the main idea and find definitions of important facts and terms.

Then Teacher A broke down reading to find the main ideas into the following steps:

1. Read chapter once.
2. Ask "What is this chapter about?"
3. Read subtitles.
4. Turn subtitles into a 'what' question.
5. Find main ideas.

Next, she wrote the steps for reading to find definitions of important facts and terms:

1. Skim chapter to find words in dark print or italics.
2. Read that sentence to define the word.
3. Read subheadings under pictures or charts.
4. Determine the idea of illustrations.
5. Write these definitions of facts and terms.

Teacher B wanted to teach his learners how to brush their teeth. He decided to review holding the brush and moving it with them. These are the steps he wrote:

1. Use the hand you write with.
2. Place the brush between your thumb and index finger so that the end of the handle is in your palm.
3. Slide thumb up handle toward bristles.
4. Hold handle with other fingers.
5. Move brush up and down.

Next, Teacher B wanted his class to learn the applications of brushing teeth. He noted that brushing teeth massaged the gums, removed plaque and controlled bad breath. Finally, Teacher B wanted to be sure his learners knew how to brush their teeth so he wrote:

1. Moisten brush.
2. Apply toothpaste.
3. Brush upper outside surfaces.
4. Brush upper inside surfaces.
5. Brush upper chewing surfaces.
6. Spit.
7. Repeat 3-6 for lower teeth.
8. Rinse with glass of water.
9. Brush teeth.

Teacher C wanted his learners to learn how to add 'ing' to words with long and short vowels. He decided that he'd review the vowel patterns with the learners so he wrote:

1. CVC = short vowel.
2. CVCE = long vowel.
3. CVVC = long vowel.

The most obvious application of adding 'ing' to a word was improved spelling in writing assignments. But Teacher C thought he would include a reading application as well. Then he wrote how to do the skill:

1. If CVC, double final 'c' and add 'ing'.
2. If CVCE, drop 'e', add 'ing'.
3. If CVCC add 'ing'.

He planned to have his learners practice on individual word lists, then move on to discriminating mistakes in sentences, and finally to writing their own sentences using 'ing'. He thought about how he would reteach the skill steps as a summary at the end of class.

Teacher D was very enthusiastic about the new Social Studies unit that would investigate the westward expansion of the United States. She had planned ways to interest the children. The first skill she selected to teach was mapping the pioneer trails. She wanted to review the skill of sketching a map with her class first so she wrote:

1. Divide paper into quarters with ruler and faint pencil lines.
2. Start in upper right hand quarter.
3. Use model on board which is divided into quarters.
4. Look at model.
5. Sketch lightly.
6. Look at sketch.
7. Repeat until first quarter of map is complete.
8. Continue working in second quarter, fourth quarter then third quarter.
9. Redraw map over light sketch lines.

Next, Teacher D wanted to give the students some applications of mapping trails. She made the following list:

a. Follow a trail using a geological survey map.
b. Make a map of a trail you used in the woods or park.

Having diagnosed her learners as having a weakness in regrouping skills when subtracting two digit numbers, Teacher E wrote the following review steps of naming numbers:

1. One's place is first place on right.
2. Name 0-9.
3. Ten's place is second place from right.
4. Name 10, 20, 30 . . . 90.
5. For 20-90 name ten's number, then one's number.
6. 11-19 have their unique names but still mean 1 ten and some ones.
7. Name numbers 1-99.

Then Teacher E wanted her learners to know that they could subtract any smaller number from any larger number if they could regroup. She wrote the following skill steps for regrouping:

1. Start with one's column. Do you need to regroup?
2. If no, subtract ones.
3. If yes, regroup a ten from the ten's column.
4. Subtract ones.
5. Subtract tens.

Then Teacher E thought about ways her learners could practice the new skill. She decided that they could use the practice examples in the text and then do some examples involving money.

**Checking Out Your Content Organization Discriminations**

To obtain your pre-training Content Organization discrimination score, complete the table below. Write down your ratings of the content of the five lessons and subtract the difference between yours and the given ratings. Add these differences and divide the sum by 5 to obtain your Content Organization discrimination score.

| Contents | Ratings | Your Ratings | | Difference (Deviation from Raters) |
|---|---|---|---|---|
| A: Outlining | 1.0 | – _____ | = | _____ |
| B: Brushing Teeth | 3.0 | – _____ | = | _____ |
| C: Adding "ing" | 5.0 | – _____ | = | _____ |
| D: Mapping Trails | 2.0 | – _____ | = | _____ |
| E: Regrouping | 4.0 | – _____ | = | _____ |
| | | Total | = | _____ |

$$\frac{\phantom{xxxxxxx}}{5} = \underline{\phantom{xxxxxxxx}}$$

Pre-Training
Content
Organization
Discrimination
Score

On the average, teachers deviate about one and one-half levels (1.5) from the trained raters on rating content organizing skills. While a score of 1.5 might not seem that significant, it means that you may be rating a "minimally effective" content organization (3.0) as "extremely effective" or "very ineffective."

At this point, you may be curious to find out how these ratings were determined. The outlining lesson seemed good, and yet it received a very low rating of 1.0. That is because Teacher A only planned the content of the **review** skills for the learners. She never actually wrote the steps of outlining. Teacher D's mapping content rated a 2.0 because she only wrote the content she would **review** and the applications of mapping trails to **overview** her skill. Teacher B's content on teeth brushing earned a rating of 3.0 because it included the content to be **reviewed** and **overviewed** as well as the content of how to do the skill for the **presentation**. Teacher E's content on regrouping skills rated 4.0 because she wrote **review** content, **overview** content and **presentation** content as well as ways the learners could practice the skill in the **exercise**. The most complete skill content was Teacher C's at 5.0. First, he wrote the **review** steps of naming vowel patterns; then he wrote the reading and writing applications of the skill for his **overview**. For the **presentation**, he wrote the skill steps of adding 'ing' and for the **exercise** he wrote the ways the learners could repeat and apply the new skills. Finally, he planned the content of a **summary**.

Martha put her pencil down reluctantly. As she looked around, she realized that she was the last one to finish the pre-test. Using Dr. Bollas' instructions, she obtained her discrimination score.

"You think there's any hope for a 1.8 discriminator, Dr. Bollas?" Martha questioned.

"That's not much worse than my 1.5," Peggy joined in.

"Hey, listen, I've got you all beat with a 2.0," George said.

"You're worried because you didn't do well on the pre-test," responded Dr. Bollas.

"We don't come off looking very good!"

"We told you we didn't know anything about lesson plans!"

"Yeah — and we **don't**!"

"That's right where you will begin. You want to be able to write good lesson plans. That's your long range goal. To reach that goal, you want to be able to write good content. This is your goal for today's seminar." Dr. Bollas indicated the following model on the chalkboard. "Today's goal is to understand what review, overview, presentation, exercise and summary consist of — to learn the ROPES — and to understand the content of each of these lesson parts."

**LESSON PLANNING SKILLS**

| Content Organization | Reviewing | Overviewing | Presenting | Exercising | Summarizing |
|---|---|---|---|---|---|

Perhaps you are beginning to understand what "organizing your content" really means. After taking the pre-test, you realize that there is specific information that learners need to learn about the new skills. You recognize that **what** you teach — content — is just as important as **how** you teach — methods. It is the marriage of content and methods that ensures your ability to write effective lesson plans. This chapter will help you investigate how to organize that content. You have learned that the most complete organization includes the content of a Review, Overview, Presentation, Exercise and Summary. Remembering the acronym **ROPES** will help you organize your content more effectively. When you have completed this chapter, you will be able to use ROPES to organize your content.

Lesson planning is the integration of your content and methods.

One of the first tasks of teaching is to **diagnose** the learners. Every group of learners brings its unique assets and deficits to the classroom. It is important to diagnose so that you can fully understand the skills the learners need to be taught. Begin by identifying a skills deficit your learners have. Select five successive skills within this deficit area. The skills should be simple enough to be taught in a week of five lessons. If you do not have learners to diagnose, choose any five sequential skills within your own specialty area. You will use these 5 skills throughout this text to help you learn lesson planning skills.

A skill is what you want your learners to be able to do. Writing a compound sentence, mixing a solution, weighing in grams and multiplying two mixed fractions are examples of skills you may want your learners to be able to do. Think carefully about the skills you select. If you are not sure that you can select five sequential skills, choose from the following examples:

Research Skills
1. Alphabetizing by first two letters.
2. Finding terms in the dictionary.
3. Defining terms from the dictionary.
4. Using the index of an encyclopedia to find page number.
5. Finding the answer to a "who" question in the encyclopedia.

Number Sentence Skills
1. $x + a = b$ $(x + 2 = 5)$.
2. $a + x = b$ $(2 + x = 5)$.
3. $x = a + b$ $(x = 2 + 5)$.
4. $x - a = b$ $(x\ 2 = 5)$.
5. $b - x = a$ $(5 - x = 2)$.

_____ Skills

1. _____

2. _____

3. _____

4. _____

5. _____

### Reviewing Contingency Skills

One of the first things you should plan is what to **review** before you teach the new skill. Ask yourself **"What other skills do my learners need to be able to do before they can do the new skill?"** For example, to write a correct sentence, your learners need to be able to write or print, spell and identify the subject and predicate. To multiply by a two-digit number, the learners need to have addition and regrouping skills. The beginning of the lesson is an appropriate time to review these **contingency skills** which your students have already learned. The skill you taught the previous day may be a contingency skill or closely related to the new skill so that you will want to review that skill. The learners may have learned the contingency skill last year. In any case, before you begin to teach the new skill, you should review any contingency skills.

## LESSON PLANNING SKILLS

Content
Organization      Reviewing

⟱

Content      Contingency
Skill Steps

## Preparing for Reviewing

Martha was not sure what skill she should select. She hadn't seen her class yet so she had no idea what skills they needed. She thought back to the classroom observations she had made in her sophomore year at the Campus School. "The kids in that class sure could have used some writing skills! For one thing, their penmanship was incredibly bad! Their papers looked as if a bunch of chickens had walked across them."

Martha tapped her pencil on her desk nervously. "I know kids are supposed to learn those skills in the first grade, but that class never did! Some of them couldn't even hold a pencil correctly. Yeah! That's what I'll do. I'll use printing skills for today's seminar. Who knows? Maybe this year's class will need those skills too."

Dr. Bollas had provided curriculum materials for the seminar students. Martha found a text on penmanship and several penmanship workbooks. Using these to help her, Martha listed the printing skills she thought she could teach in a week. Then she wrote the contingency skills of each skill.

Using Martha's sample, take the time now to list the contingency skills of the five successive skills you selected to write lesson plans for.

| SKILL | CONTINGENCY SKILLS |
|---|---|
| Printing Skills | Hold a pencil. Control a pencil. |
| 1.  Print "i,l,t" | Make vertical and horizontal lines. |
| 2.  Print "c,e,o,s" | Make circles and horizontal lines. |
| 3.  Print "a,b,d,p" | Make circles and vertical lines. |
| 4.  Print "g,h,j,f,m,n,q,r,u" | Make circles and half circles. |
| 5.  Print "k,v,w,x,y,z" | Make slanted, vertical and horizontal lines. |

## SKILL                    CONTINGENCY SKILLS

Skills

1. _____     _____

2. _____     _____

3. _____     _____

4. _____     _____

5. _____     _____

Identify the contingency skills

The review is a significant part of your lesson plan. You will use the review to diagnose where the learners are.

"Can they perform the contingency skills?"

"Do you need to teach a simpler skill or one that is more complex?"

After you teach your learners how to do the contingency skill, you will answer these questions when the learners perform the contingency skill. You will be able to observe the level of the skills that your learners have.

When you review, you can diagnose your learners.

## Overviewing Applications

When you **overview** the new skill with your learners, you are in effect, **giving them a reason for learning the new skill**. You know what **your** reason is for teaching the new skill. It is one link in the chain of skills that make up your curriculum. Your students need to learn how to multiply before they learn how to divide. Unless they learn to multiply, they will have to write long, long columns of addition. Multiplication is much faster than addition. If Martha's students do not learn how to print an i, l or t, she knows that they will not be able to write legible words, sentences or paragraphs. But she has a perspective on the problem that her learners do not have. She will try to share that perspective in the overview.

### LESSON PLANNING SKILLS

| Content | Reviewing | Overviewing |
|---|---|---|
| Organization |  |  |
| Content | Contingency Skill Steps | Skill Applications |

## Bridging the Learning Gap

To give the learners a perspective of the new skill, you must first correct the discrepancy between **where your learners think they are** and **where you know they are**. How many times have the learners said:

"We learned that last year. Not again!"

"We know how to do that!"

"This is useless! Why do we have to learn this?"

Yet you know very well that they need to relearn the skills. That is why you have planned to teach them. You could confront your learners head to head and demand they learn the skill. Or you could use your finesse and teach your learners the difference between what they think they know and what they really know. Then you might hear your learners say:

"Ours doesn't look like yours!"

"Yours looks better! How come?"

"Teach us to do that!"

Martha knew that she could not just walk into a classroom and tell the learners that they were going to learn how to print. They would laugh at her! After all, they learned that way back in the first grade — or so they thought. She would never be able to reach her objective of having her learners write legibly. Using the format "If you learn to print, then you can_____," she made a list of ways her learners could apply the skills.

Printing Skills   Applications:
1.  If you learn to print, then you can write words, sentences, paragraphs.
2.  If you learn to print, then you can draw posters.
3.  If you learn to print, then you can draw maps and charts.

Try writing a list of **applications** of the skills for which you are planning a lesson. These applications will be reasons for your learners to master the new skills.

_____ Skills    Applications:

1. _____

2. _____

3. _____

4. _____

5. _____

Your overview really involves teaching the applications or uses of the skill to the learners. It reminds the learners that what they are learning today is just a small piece of tomorrow's larger picture. In addition, the overview helps them to diagnose themselves in relation to that picture. When it comes down to the wire, Martha may find that the learners are very concerned about their lack of printing ability. She may hear them say:

"Mine always looks so messy! Uck!"

"I'm just a slob, I guess!"

"You think I'll be able to do it right, huh?"

Where the review helps the teacher diagnose the learners' readiness to learn the new skill, the overview helps the learners diagnose their own readiness to learn that skill. Once the teacher and the learners are aware of where the learners stand, they are ready for the presentation of the new skill.

When you overview the new skill, your learners can diagnose themselves in relation to the new skill.

After you have written the content for the review and overview of the skill you plan to teach, you are ready to attack the **presentation**. You will teach your learners **how to perform the skill**. To do this, you need to break that skill down into the steps your learners take to perform the skill. This is critical to the success of your planning and delivery as far as your learners are concerned. As simple as it sounds, it takes practice to be able to break down the skills you teach into learner-size steps. How many times have you heard your learners say:

"What do I do first?"

"We don't know where to begin!"

"What do we do next?"

What your learners are really asking you for are the steps they need to perform the skill successfully.

### LESSON PLANNING SKILLS

| Content Organization | Reviewing | ▶ | Overviewing | ▶ | Presenting |
|---|---|---|---|---|---|
| | ⬇ | | ⬇ | | ⬇ |
| Content | Contingency Skill Steps | | Skill Applications | | Skill Steps |

Martha knew that she would have to eliminate bad habits her learners had accumulated over the years. That meant that she had to start back at the very beginning. She took a look at the first printing skills.

"Mmmmm. Printing 'i', 'l' and 't'," Martha said to herself. "I grouped those letters together because they all use vertical and horizontal lines. I guess now I'm ready to break down the printing of each letter into steps."

The first thing Martha did was to write the skill as a **last** step.

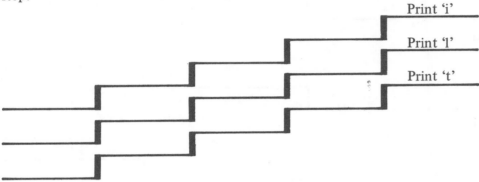

Then she wrote the very **first** step the learners would take to print the letter. In this case, Martha's first step was where to start the letter.

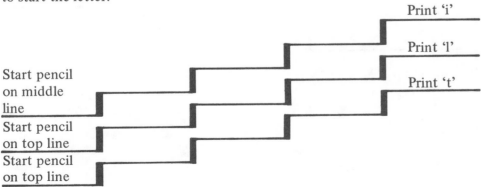

Using your list of skills, write the first and last step your learners would take to perform each of the five skills you selected. Use Martha's sample lesson as an example to write the skill steps.

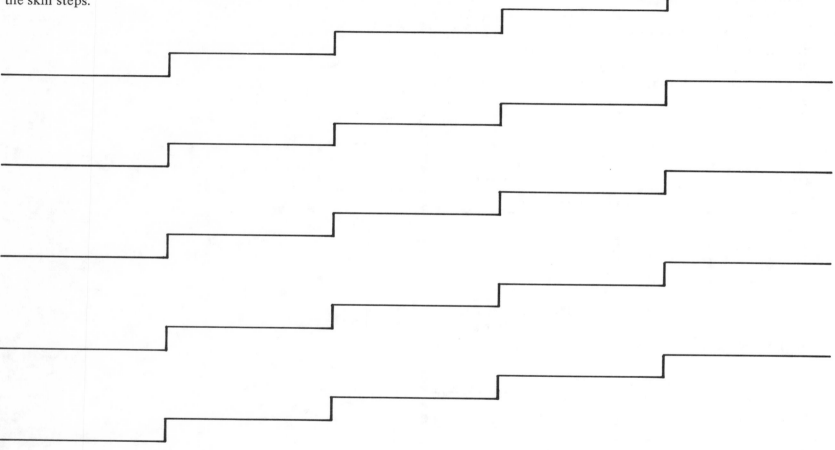

Martha then filled in the intermediary skill steps. These are the steps her learners will take to go from the first step to the last step. Martha asked herself, "If my learners start on the middle line, what do they have to do next to print an 'i'?"

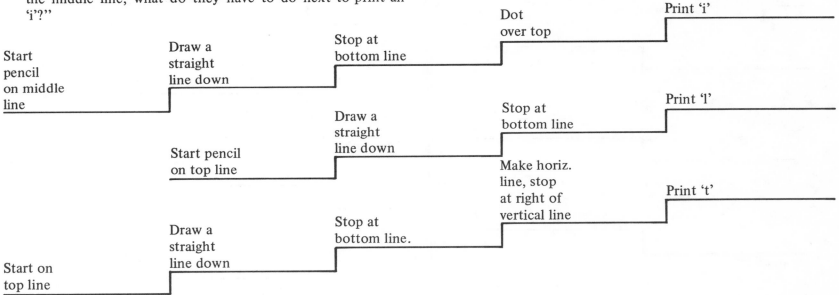

You'll note that Martha has only developed four steps for teaching her learners to print an 'l'. The key to developing skill steps is not to stick with an arbitrary number but, instead, to make sure that no "gaps" exist between separate steps!

You should be able to fill in the remaining skill steps of your five skills. Use Martha's sample as a model. Ask yourself: "If I (1st step), what do I do next to be able to (last step)?"

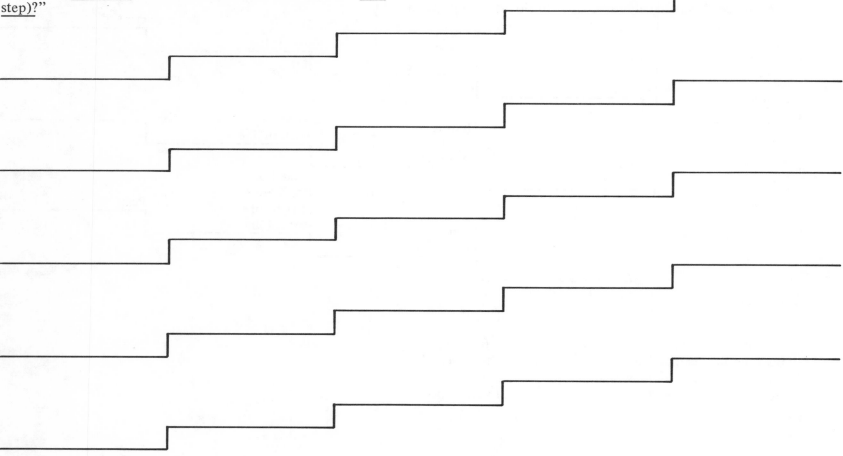

To check her steps, Martha actually performed what she had written. When she found that she was doing something in addition to what she had written, she added another step. For example, she had first written the fourth step of printing a 't' simply as "cross the 't' with a horizontal line."

BEFORE:

Cross 't' with horizontal line

Print 't'

Stop at bottom line

Draw a straight line down

Start on top line

But when Martha performed the steps herself, she found that she had not indicated where to start or finish the cross of the t. So she added another step to her program.

Make horizontal line at right of vertical line

Print 't'

Start cross to middle left of vertical line

New Step

Stop at bottom line

Draw a straight line down

Start on top line

You should do the same with your steps to evaluate their completeness. When you are teaching the presentation of your lesson, you will want to make sure that all your learners will be able to perform the new skill. They will not be successful if you have left any skill steps out of your program.

Breaking down a skill into skill steps is critical to reorganizing your content. The steps tell your learners exactly what to do and in what order. If you write out the skill steps completely, then the learners can successfully perform the steps. If the skill steps are incomplete, the chances are that the learners will be unsuccessful.

Martha may hear some grumbling like: "Why do we have to do this?" But if her learners work with the steps, they will see how much better their printing looks.

"Hey! Look at mine! It looks so **good**!"

Skill steps give your learners direction.

**Writing Skill Steps for the Contingency Skills of the Review**

Martha can also break down the contingency skills of the review into skill steps. Again, the steps tell the learners exactly what they have to do to perform the skill correctly. Below is an example of how Martha broke down the contingency skills her learners needed to review into skill steps.

Review Skill

Lesson #1
Print "i, l, t"

Contingency Skills:
**Making Horizontal and Vertical Lines**

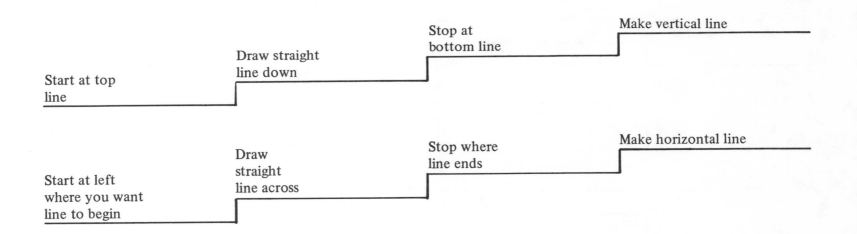

Start at top line
Draw straight line down
Stop at bottom line
Make vertical line

Start at left where you want line to begin
Draw straight line across
Stop where line ends
Make horizontal line

**68   Using a Model to Write the Skill Steps of the Contingency Skills**

As a further practice exercise, write the skill steps of the contingency skills for your review. Some may already have been written for the previous presentation. Write the skill steps for only those contingency skills which you haven't broken down.

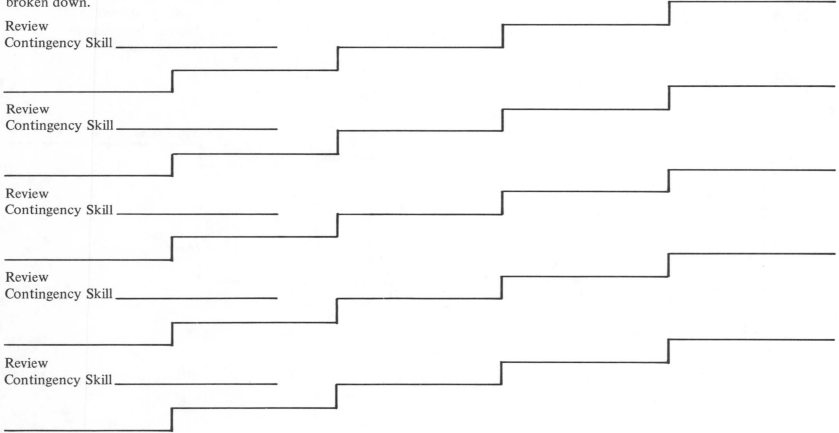

Review
Contingency Skill _____

Review
Contingency Skill _____

Review
Contingency Skill _____

Review
Contingency Skill _____

Review
Contingency Skill _____

At this point, you may want to review what you have learned about organizing your content for delivery. The first part of your lesson is spent on a **review**. You will first have to identify the contingency skills of the skill you plan to teach. Writing the skill steps of these contingency skills tells you what content to deliver in the **review**. When you deliver the **review**, you are diagnosing your learners' readiness to learn the new skill. You may say "My kids are ready for multiplication because they know their number facts and how to regroup."

Next, you will **overview** the skill. Identifying the applications of the new skill makes it possible to motivate the learners to learn the new skill. You want your learners to diagnose themselves in relation to the new skill. Your learners may say "I want to learn how to throw a ball so that I can play baseball."

To prepare your **presentation**, you realize that your skill needs to be broken down into steps. Again, you need all of the steps of the skill so that your learners know just what to do. Before long you may hear your learners say,"I bet I can do that!"

The next part of your lesson plan organization is the **exercise**. The learners need the opportunity to perform the new skill. The learners will have already been taught how to perform the steps of the skill in the **presentation**. They may have had an opportunity to do the skill at least once. But once is not enough. The **exercise** of the lesson does not introduce any new content but **involves the learners in repeated use of the new skill**. The skill will be performed by itself. Then the learners will do exercises which have them use the new skill in conjunction with other skills. The more times you can involve your learners in using the new skill, the more you increase their chances of being able to master the new skill. A variety of practice materials and applications will keep the learning exciting.

| Content Organization | Reviewing ▶ | Overviewing ▶ | Presenting ▶ | Exercising |
|---|---|---|---|---|
| | ⬇ | ⬇ | ⬇ | ⬇ |
| Content | Contingency Skill Steps | Skill Application | Skill Steps | Skill Steps |

## Using a Model to Write the Needed Materials

Martha continued to plan how she would organize her lessons to teach printing skills. She knew that her learners would need a lot of practice. Breaking years of bad habits was not going to be easy. The content of the **exercise** was the same as for the presentation, but she needed a number of ways to help them practice the skill steps.

"What do my learners use to print?" thought Martha. "Let's see . . . they could use pencils, pens or crayons. Maybe even magic markers or paint. Of course, they print on paper," she continued, "But it could be plain or lined paper."

What Martha was actually doing was expanding the list of materials her learners could use to repeat their printing skills. Use Martha's list of materials as a model to make your own list of materials that your learners would use to perform the skills you selected.

Materials

Printing Skills

pencil, pen, crayon, magic marker, paint
plain or lined paper, construction paper
newsprint

Materials

——————————— Skills

_____

_____

_____

_____

_____

Then Martha selected the materials she would use to have her learners practice the first skill. She tried to choose materials that would be easiest for her learners to use as she wanted them to be successful when they performed the skill.

Materials

Painting Skills

Print 'i'
_____
pencil and lined paper

Which materials would you select to have your learners use to perform your first skill? Remember that you want to select materials that your learners can use with success.

Materials

_____ Skills

First Skill:_____

_____

Second Skill:_____

_____

Third Skill:_____

_____

Fourth Skill:_____

_____

Fifth Skill:_____

_____

You have expanded and selected the materials your learners will use to perform each new skill. The next step is to investigate where your learners can apply the new skills. These application situations will suggest ways for the learners to practice the new skill with other skills. For example, instead of just printing letters, Martha's learners will use the letters to make words, sentences and paragraphs. Then they could use the words and sentences to make posters, charts or maps. These are the same applications that Martha used when she planned the **overview**.

Printing Skills        Applications:
1. If you learn to print letters, then you can write words, sentences or paragraphs.
2. If you learn to print letters, then you can draw posters.
3. If you learn to print letters, then you can draw maps and charts.

Martha took a look at the first printing skill she had planned to teach: Printing 'i, l, t.' "Since the learners will not have learned to print the other letters correctly, they won't be able to write paragraphs. Even sentences will be difficult!" As she looked over the list of applications, she realized that there were many different skills involved in using the applications of printing 'i, l, t.' She had to first identify what skills were involved in doing the application. Second, she needed to check off which of these skills her learners could perform.

Printing Skills        Applications:
1. Print letters so you can write words (printing skills, spelling skills). √
2. Print letters so you can write sentences (printing skills, writing skills). √
3. Print letters so you can write paragraphs (printing skills, writing skills).
4. Print letters so you can draw posters (printing skills, measuring skills, drawing skills).
5. Print letters so you can draw maps and charts (printing skills, measuring skills, drawing skills, coloring skills).

**74   Using a Model to Write the Content of Exercise**

Examine the applications you wrote in the **overview**. List the skills that your learners use when they perform each of these applications. Then check those skills which your learners have already acquired.

_____ Skills          Applications:

1._____

_____

2._____

_____

3._____

_____

4._____

_____

5._____

_____

**Teaching the Exercise**

You have always known how important it is for the learners to practice the new learning. Practice does make perfect provided the **exercise** is meaningful. Martha now understands that her learners should use the materials needed to perform the particular skill. She will **select materials for the exercise that they will have success with.** Then she will study the applications of the skill to determine what other skills the learners use when they practice the new skill. If the practice includes skills the learners have not learned, they will fail. So Martha will **select the applications which use the new skill in conjunction with skills the learners have already mastered.** Then Martha may hear her learners say:

"So that's how it works!"

"Now I can do it!"

"That's NEAT!"

When you have the learners exercise they have an opportunity to practice the skill.

The final part of your lesson is a **summary**. This gives you **another opportunity to review the new skill with your learn-ers.** They may have forgotten a step or not fully understood a part of what they were doing in the exercise. You summarize the steps of performing the skill. Then you can diagnose where your learners are in relation to what you have taught. Your learners can use the summary to diagnose themselves in relation to what they have learned.

| Content | Reviewing | ▶ | Overviewing | ▶ | Presenting | ▶ | Exercising | ▶ | Summarizing |
|---|---|---|---|---|---|---|---|---|---|
| Organization | ⬇ | | ⬇ | | ⬇ | | ⬇ | | ⬇ |
| Content | Contingency Skill Steps | | Skill Application | | Skill Steps | | Skill Steps | | Skill Steps |

## Summarizing is Reviewing

As can be seen, summarizing serves the same function as reviewing. Where you reviewed the contingency skills to begin the organization of your content, now you use the skill steps from your presentation to summarize your content. Just as the review did, your summary provides you with an opportunity to diagnose where your learners are in relation to what you have taught. Most importantly, the summary provides your learners with the opportunity to diagnose themselves in relation to what they have learned.

When you summarize, the learners have an opportunity to review what they have learned.

## Summarizing is Diagnosing

When Martha plans her summary, she will reteach the steps of the skill. She wants to focus her learners' attention again on the steps of the skill. To do this, she will go back to steps she developed for the presentation of the skill. Then Martha will want to have her learners do the skill once more. This will be another opportunity for the learners to perform the skill. But more importantly, it will give Martha another opportunity to diagnose her learners. She wants to know if they are doing the skill correctly before she teaches the next skill.

You have just learned how to use ROPES to organize the content of the lesson. Take the time to read the summary below. You should be more confident in your use of ROPES to organize your content.

**R**eview.    **Identify the contingency skills** the learners need to perform the new skill successfully. To write the content of the contingency skill, you need to **break down the contingency skill into skill steps.**

**O**verview.    **Identify the applications** of how the learners will use the new skill. To write the content of the overview, you will **select the applications that are relevant to the learners.**

**P**resenta-    **Break down the skill into skill steps** the learn-
tion.    ers will take to perform the skill.

**E**xercise.    **Identify the materials** the learners will use to perform the skill. Then **identify the skills** within the applications of the overview. Finally, **choose skills the learners already can do.**

**S**ummary.    **Review how to do the skill** once more, using the skill steps from the presentation.

## POST-TRAINING ASSESSMENT OF CONTENT ORGANI-ZATION SKILLS

### Using Your Content Organization Skills

Select a new skill or use the content you used in the pre-test. Write an outline of the skill content as you would teach it.

### CONTENT OUTLINE

Skill: _____

_____

_____

_____

_____

_____

_____

_____

_____

_____

_____

_____

_____

_____

_____

_____

Your next task will ask you to discriminate the organization of five content outlines. Again, some lessons are more complete than others. Rate these outlines on a scale from 1.0 to 5.0 where 1.0 is the least complete organization and 5.0 is the most complete organization.

1.0  Very Ineffective

2.0  Ineffective

3.0  Minimally Effective

4.0  Very Effective

5.0  Extremely Effective

If you feel a lesson falls between two levels on the scale, you may rate it as 1.5, 2.5, 3.5 or 4.5. For example, suppose the lesson plan seemed better than "minimally effective," but not quite "very effective." You would rate it a 3.5. You may use any rating more than once.

Teacher A had diagnosed her learners as needing measuring or "ruler" skills. She planned to teach them how to measure inches first. But first she wanted to review how to find numbers using a number line with the learners.

1. Find 0.
2. One space to right = 1.
3. Two spaces to right = 2.
4. Three spaces to right = 3.
5. Repeat until twelve spaces to right = 12.
6. Find numbers 1-12 on a number line.

Next, Teacher A wrote the application of measuring in inches:
Follow directions to make designs and models out of paper.
Find out how long to cut string or ribbon for decorations.

Then she wrote the skill steps the learners needed to do the skill:

1. Put the zero end of the ruler at one end of what you are measuring.
2. Move to the right to find the number opposite the other end of what you are measuring.
3. Read or write that number which is the measure in inches.

For exercises, Teacher A planned to have the learners measure common objects and then apply the new skill by measuring and cutting shapes out of construction paper. Finally, she planned to summarize the three steps of using a ruler.

Teacher B was concerned about how poorly her learners threw a softball on the playground at recess. She decided to teach them how to throw. First, she wanted to review how to throw underhand. She wrote:

1. Hold ball in palm of hand facing up.
2. Bring ball back behind you.
3. Step with opposite foot as ball comes forward.
4. Release ball where you want it to go.
5. Throw underhand.

Next, she would show the learners applications of throwing overhand in softball and baseball. Then she wrote the skill steps of throwing overhand:

1. Hold ball with four fingers spread on top, thumb pointing down.
2. Bring the ball back behind ear.
3. Step with opposite foot.
4. Snap wrist.
5. Follow through where you want ball to go.
6. Throw overhand.

Then Teacher B decided that the best way to practice the steps was to throw at a target and then apply the skills in a game of softball.

Teacher C was in the midst of planning the skills he would teach in the geometry unit. One of the first skills he would teach was finding the area of a triangle. He liked this skill because it was so easy to prove the formula to the learners. Cutting any rectangle into two equal triangles always delighted the students. They could really understand $A=\frac{1}{2}bh$. Teacher C wanted to make sure the learners could multiply $\frac{1}{2}$ times two whole numbers so he wrote:

1. Put whole numbers over one.
2. Put two multiplication signs between the three numbers.
3. Slash if possible.
4. Multiply 3 numerators for answer numerator.
5. Multiply 3 denominators for answer denominator.
6. Divide answer numerator by answer denominator for mixed number answer.
7. Multiply three fractions.

Teacher D wanted her learners to learn the skill of finding answers to research questions in an encyclopedia. In social studies, Teacher D's class was studying Colonial America. She had identified the names of leaders she wanted the learners to know. It would be easiest to find the answers to 'who' questions in an encyclopedia. She wrote the steps to making alphabetical order:

1.  Find the words that begin with 'a'.
2.  If more than one, look at second letter.
3.  If necessary, look at third letter in 'a' words.
4.  Number the order of the 'a' words.
5.  Find the words that begin with 'b'.
6.  Continue as in numbers 2 through 4.
7.  Alphabetize a list of words.

Then Teacher D wanted her learners to see other sources in the library, where they could find the answers to other questions, by using alphabetical order skills.

Teacher E had diagnosed her reading class as needing to be able to state the story problem. This was one step toward improving their reading comprehension. As a contingency skill, she would first teach the learners to find the sentence in the reading that states the story problem:

1. Read story.
2. Ask "What is wrong?"
3. Find the sentence that states what is wrong or story problem.

She decided that she could show her readers how to state the solution to the story problem or even write their own stories around a problem as an overview of stating the story problem. Then she wrote the steps to stating the story problem:

1. Find the sentence that states what is wrong.
2. Read the sentence carefully.
3. Ask yourself "What is wrong?"
4. State answer to story problem in own words.

Some of you may be quite anxious to see how well you did on the post-training assessment. Use the table below to check your ratings. Write the difference between your ratings and the given ratings. Add these differences and divide by 5 to obtain your content organization discrimination score.

| Content Outline | | Ratings | | Your Ratings | | Differences (Deviations) |
|---|---|---|---|---|---|---|
| A: | Measuring Skills | 5.0 | − | _____ | = | _____ |
| B: | Throwing Skills | 4.0 | − | _____ | = | _____ |
| C: | Geometry Skills | 1.0 | − | _____ | = | _____ |
| D: | Researching Skills | 2.0 | − | _____ | = | _____ |
| E: | Stating Problem | 3.0 | − | _____ | = | _____ |
| | | | | Total | = | _____ | = |

$$\frac{\phantom{xxxx}}{5}$$

Post-training
Content Organization
Discrimination
Score

If your discrimination score was more than .5, then you should go back and reread Chapter Two and redo the exercises. If your score was .5 or less, then you are ready to go on.

Now you would probably like to know how the post-test ratings were determined. Teacher C's Geometry content rated 1.0 because he had only the skill steps of the **review** skill. Teacher D's researching content rated 2.0 because she had only the content of the **review** and applications of the **overview**. At 3.0, Teacher E's stating the problem content contained the content for the **review**, **overview** and **presentation**. Teacher B's overhand throwing skills were rated 4.0 because they included the content of **review**, **overview**, **presentation** and **exercise**. The five elements of ROPES found in A's measuring content earned her a perfect 5.0 rating.

1.0  Content for any **one** part of ROPES

2.0  Content for any **two** parts of ROPES

3.0  Content for any **three** parts of ROPES

4.0  Content for any **four** parts of ROPES

5.0  Content for **all five** parts of ROPES

Because you now understand how the ratings are given, you can go back to your own content outline in the pre- and post-test that you wrote and give yourself a rating. Remember that your content should be organized around ROPES. The skill steps of the contingency skills and the new skill, the applications of the new skill, the ways or materials used to practice and apply the new skill are the content of a well-organized lesson.

_____ Pre-Test
Content Organization
Communication
Score

_____ Post-Test
Content Organization
Communication
Score

You have learned how to organize the content of your lessons using ROPES. When you use ROPES, you can answer the question "What do I teach my learners?" You can apply ROPES to your own learning.

"What skills do I need to **review** in order to be able to do the new skill?"

"What are the applications of this skill so that I can **overview** the skill?"

"What are the skill steps I need to do when I **present** the skill to myself?"

"What materials do I use and with what skills can I practice the new skill for the **exercise**?"

"How can I **summarize** the steps I have learned?"

Many times you have tried to succeed at learning without a teacher or with a teacher who is poorly organized. ROPES will help you organize the content so that you can learn new skills independently.

ROPES can help you organize your own learning.

## Organizing Your Content

The seminar was over. The students had been given their post-test scores and assignments for the next seminar.

"Hey! That really wasn't too bad after all," said Martha to Peggy.

"See? I told you you'd learn something. What did you get on your post-test, anyway?" Peggy asked.

Martha grinned at Peggy. "A great big .25!"

Peggy looked disgusted. "After all that complaining . . . Honestly, you're too much, Martha! I'm not going to pay any more attention to all that noise you make. Listen, I only got a .4."

"Well, I'm glad I don't have to do that section over. I've never had a teacher that made you go back and relearn stuff the way Dr. Bollas did today," Martha said. "Did you see how upset Anne and John were about not being able to go on with the rest of us?"

"Uh huh — and just because they didn't get a .5 discrimination score or lower," added Peggy. "I think that's a little tough!"

"Oh, I don't know if it was so tough . . . They really didn't get the stuff at all. They'll really get lost if they go on without knowing this stuff. Breaking down the skill into steps is pretty tricky. Besides, we've been kind of spoiled. You know that nobody takes ed. courses seriously. Maybe we all have to learn to work a little harder."

# 3

## CHAPTER 3: PREPARING YOUR METHODS
### TELL-SHOW-DO

**Experiencing Teaching Methods**

There are as many different kinds of teaching as there are teachers. Think back to some of the teaching we experienced as students. Some of our teachers taught poorly. Let's face it! Their classes were dull and boring. These teachers talked to us . . . and talked . . . and talked!

Most of our teachers had their good days and their bad days. Neither great all the time nor boring, they were just "okay." These teachers did the best that they could with what they knew. We sensed that they were trying and we respected them because they were sincere.

A few of our teachers were outstanding. Their teaching delivery was one great performance after another. We learned in spite of ourselves. These superb teachers knew something about teaching that our other teachers did not. Clock watching wasn't necessary. One activity followed another, each day better than the one before. We know some of the things that these special teachers did. They not only told us what they wanted us to do and how to do it, but they showed us. And, most importantly, they provided us with an opportunity to do it ourselves. If we did not do it, we really didn't learn it. You want to be that special kind of teacher.

Good teachers let their learners perform the new learning.

The teaching delivery you plan can make you that special kind of teacher. Knowing what the learners need to learn, you develop that content using ROPES. Planning your lesson to **tell**, **show** and **do**, ROPES helps you plan an effective teaching delivery.

"What do I **tell** my learners and how do I **tell** them?"

"What do I **show** my learners and how do I **show** them?"

"What do I have my learners **do** and how will I have them **do** it?"

These are the questions that must be answered when you prepare the teaching delivery.

**Preparing to Learn Teaching Methods**

"How goes the war, George?" Martha and George were both running up the steps of Dana Hall for their second seminar.

"Not bad, Martha! Not bad at all. I'm teaching every day now," George said proudly. "What? How come? I'm still at the back of the room observing!" Martha was confused.

"That's because you're at the Campus School. They do things by the book there, don't they?" Martha nodded her head. "Well, up at old North School my cooperating teacher met me at the door the first day. And I haven't seen him since."

"Really? What did you do? I mean . . . all those kids! I would have panicked for sure!"

George smiled and said nonchalantly, "Well, at first I thought I was being thrown into the lion's den. Then I decided since there was hope for Daniel, why not me? So I started teaching and you know what? I wasn't half bad!"

"Better you than me! I want some more help before I get up in front of a group," replied Martha. "How about you, Peggy?"

Peggy had joined Martha and George as they talked about their experiences the first week of student teaching. "Well, I really want to learn about these methods in seminar today. I'm going to start teaching the third reading group tomorrow and I want to know what methods I should use." Peggy looked very determined. "I've got to do all I can to get good recommendations! I don't want to spend the rest of my life selling hamburgers!"

The three student teachers entered the seminar room and took their seats. The classroom hummed with news and gossip about the students' experiences. "I know you are all happy to be back together on campus," said Dr. Bollas. "It's a different world out there, isn't it?"

The students vigorously agreed with his last statement. "Today we will investigate different teaching methods you will use when you teach in the coming weeks. Let's find out what you know and what you don't know about teaching methods." Dr. Bollas drew a batch of papers out of his briefcase and said, "We will begin with a pre-test."

### Using Teaching Methods

You selected a content to teach your learners in Chapter Two. Before you outlined that content, it was assumed that you diagnosed your learners to find out where they were in relation to the content. Using ROPES, you wrote the content of the skills your learners needed to learn. Now you need to plan how you will deliver that content to the learners.

Before you begin the teaching methods module, it is important that you get an index of your ability to develop teaching methods. Accordingly, use your teaching methods in the following exercise. Choose one of the **content outlines** you developed with ROPES in Chapter Two. Outline how you would teach the content of just the **presentation** to your learners.

_____ Skills

Skill: _____

Presentation: _____

_____

_____

_____

_____

_____

_____

_____

You may have discovered that it is not so easy to outline good teaching methods. You may find yourself lapsing back to some of your old lecture methods.

"Tell them what to do first."

"Tell them what a denominator is."

"Tell them to simplify their answers."

Perhaps you have some idea of what you want to do to teach the skill, but you cannot express it so that the learners will all learn the skill.

It will probably be easier for you to recognize good teaching methods when you see them. To test your ability to discriminate teaching methods, rate the plans for teaching the review skills on the next few pages. Use a scale from 1.0 to 3.0 as follows:

1.0    Very Ineffective

2.0    Ineffective

3.0    Minimally Effective

If you feel a lesson falls between two levels on the three-point scale, you may rate it as 1.5 or 2.5. For example, if the review seems almost "minimally effective," you would give a rating of 2.5 to that delivery plan. You may use a rating more than once.

**Review:** Finding the main idea.

1. Teacher tells the class that the review skill is finding the main idea of the reading.

2. Teacher shows the first transparency which tells the first step of the skill: a) Read chapter once.

   Then shows overlay with an example from yesterday's social studies class. Teacher has learners read the chapter in the science text.

3. Teacher continues to tell the steps, gives an example on an overlay and has the learners do the step with the science text:
   a) Ask "What is this chapter about?"
   b) Read subtitles.
   c) Turn subtitles into a 'what' question.
   d) Find main idea.

**Review:**   Holding and moving a toothbrush

1.   Teacher asks a learner to stand up in front of the class and show the other learners how to hold a toothbrush.

2.   Teacher places magnetized placards of each step in random order on the chalkboard. Ask learners to write the order they would pick to do the skill.

3.   Learners take turns putting placards in order.
     a)  Use hand you write with
     b)  Place the brush between your thumb and index finger so that the end of the handle is in your palm
     c)  Slide thumb up handle toward bristles
     d)  Hold handle with other fingers
     e)  Move brush up and down

**Review:**    Short vowel and long vowel patterns

1. Teacher asks the learners to put the following words into three categories: ban, bin, but, bait, bean, bead, bone, bide, bile.

2. After several learners have explained their category system, the teacher puts up his system which is CVC, CVCE and CVVC.

3. Teacher tries to find a learner who can explain the teacher's category system to the class.

**Review**:　　Sketching a map

1.　Teacher places a flip chart in front of the class showing a model U.S. map that is divided into four quarters.

2.　Teacher points out the major points of outlining the first quarter. Teacher tells the learners the following:
   a)　Divide paper into quarters with ruler and faint pencil lines
   b)　Start lightly in upper right hand quarter
   c)　Use model on flip chart
   d)　Look at model
   e)　Sketch lightly
   f)　Look at sketch
   g)　Repeat until first quarter looks like model
   h)　Make second quarter, fourth quarter, then third quarter
   i)　Redraw map over light sketch lines

Teacher places these steps on the chalkboard.

**Review:**      Naming numbers 1-99

1.      Teacher asks learners to write down their favorite number between 0 and 100 on a scrap of paper. Then learners tell numbers and teacher makes list on chalkboard. Teacher selects all numbers less than ten and asks "What are they called?" Learner or teacher says these are the 'ones'. Teacher writes down the first two steps on chalkboard.
a)  One's place is first place on right:
b)  Name of ones: 0-9

2.      Teacher selects 10, 20, 30 . . . 90 and asks "what are they called?" Learner  or  teacher  says  these are "tens." Teacher  writes  down  next  two steps  on chalkboard:
a)  Ten's place is second place from right:
b)  Name of tens: 10, 20 . . . 90.

Then selects  all  the  numbers that have tens and ones. Teacher writes down fifth step:
c)  For 21-99 name ten's  number,  then one's number.

Learners  take  turns  reading  their  numbers from the board while teacher points to ten's and one's place, Teacher explains 11-19 names.

3.      Learners follow steps on chalkboard to write the names of the following: 35, 48, 64, 93, 29.

**Checking Out Your Teaching Methods Discrimination**

You may be eager to see how well you discriminated the teaching methods. Use the table below to find the difference between your ratings and the given ratings. Divide the sum of these differences by 5 to obtain your teaching methods discrimination score.

| Lesson Plan | Ratings | Your Ratings | Difference (Deviation) |
|---|---|---|---|
| A: Finding main idea | 3.0 | − ____ = | _____ |
| B: Holding a toothbrush | 2.0 | − ____ = | _____ |
| C: Vowel patterns | 1.0 | − ____ = | _____ |
| D: Map sketching | 1.0 | − ____ = | _____ |
| E: Naming numbers | 3.0 | − ____ = | _____ |
| | | Total = | _____ = _____ |

5     Pre-test
Teaching Methods
Discrimination
Score

On the average, teachers deviate about one to one and one -half levels on rating delivery preparation skills. This means that you may be rating an "ineffective" content organization (2.0) as "minimally effective" or "very ineffective." A deviation of .5 or less means that you are more closely approximating the ratings of trained raters.

You may be interested in a further explanation of how the ratings were obtained for the delivery of the review skills. Teacher C's review of vowel patterns and Teacher D's review of sketching a map received "very ineffective" ratings of 1.0. They neither **show** their learners how to do the skill steps nor do they have their learners **do** the skill steps. The only delivery methods they employ are **tell** methods. Teacher B's review lesson plan is rated 2.0 or "ineffective" because he used only **tell** and **show** methods to teach the skill steps of holding a toothbrush. He did not plan a method to have the learners **do** the skill; thus, his plan was not as effective as it could be. Teacher A's and E's lesson plans were rated effective at 3.0 because they used **tell, show** and **do** methods. Teacher A **told** the step with a transparency, she **showed** how to do the step on an overlay and then she had the learners **do** that step with their own learning.

Now you are ready to learn about **tell, show, do** teaching methods.

"Here we go again, Peggy," said Martha. "Look at that . . . 2.0! I'm getting worse instead of better."

"Ah, c'mon, don't get all hassled! That's what we're here for. Shut up and listen to the man."

Dr. Bollas was again responding to his students' expressions. "I can tell by your faces that you are concerned with your ability to discriminate teaching methods. Your long-range goal is still to learn to write a lesson plan. Last week, your goal was to learn how to organize your content." He pointed to a model he had drawn on the chalkboard. "This week we will learn about the **tell, show, do** methods of the review. That's this week's goal. First, we will begin with the tell methods.

## LESSON PLANNING SKILLS

| Content Organization | Reviewing | ► | Overviewing | ► | Presenting | ► | Exercising | ► | Summarizing |
|---|---|---|---|---|---|---|---|---|---|
| | ⇩ | | ⇩ | | ⇩ | | ⇩ | | ⇩ |
| Content | Contingency Skill Steps | | Skill Applications | | Skill Steps | | Skill Steps | | Skill Steps |
| | ⇩ | | ⇩ | | ⇩ | | ⇩ | | ⇩ |
| Methods | Telling | | Telling | | Telling | | Telling | | Telling |

### Telling Names, Definitions, Reasons and Steps

Telling is the most common source of learning. From many teachers' frames of reference, the easiest way to deliver is to **tell** the learners what they need to know. In other words, they lecture. Telling is essential but not sufficient for your teaching delivery. You tell your learners about the new learning. If they need a fact like the name of an object, you will **tell** them that it is called an "internal combustion engine." Your learners may need concepts like the definitions of new terms. You **tell** them "compression is when the piston moves up in the cylinder, squeezing the fuel and air mixture." In a like manner, you **tell** your learners about the principles that explain why things work that way when you say "the exploding gases push the piston down." **Telling** your learners how to perform the steps of a skill could include **saying** that "the first step is to check the spark plugs to see if they need replacement."

Telling methods let your learners hear what they should learn.

Examine the different kinds of learners you have in your class. The learners who are predominantly auditory listen to you intently. You tell them what to do and they do it. These learners will tend to interact in classroom discussions more than other kinds of learners. Because they are predominantly auditory, they will also learn well from written material. Your delivery will meet the needs of your auditory learners when you tell them about what they need to know.

Some learners learn best from **tell** methods.

## Telling the Learners What You Want Them to Learn

Using **tell** methods is one of your teaching delivery skills. **Tell** methods answer the question:

"What am I going to use to **tell** my class what they want or need to learn?"

For the moment, you may take the safe side and select methods which simply **tell** the learners what they are to learn. For example, there are a variety of **tell** sources available to you: you, another teacher, a learner or a guest speaker. In addition, there is a variety of equipment that can be employed by these sources to tell: an audiotape, a videotape, a record, textbook, worksheet, transparency or a poster. All of these could be used as **tell** methods. While most **tell** methods are auditory, there are some that are visual. All **tell** methods deal with words, either spoken or written.

## Practicing Identifying Tell Methods

Read the following description of part of a teaching delivery. The skill that the students are learning is finding the perimeter of a rectangle. The excerpt describes the first step of learning the skill: identifying a rectangle. The **tell** methods that are included in the excerpt are only part of the delivery. Identify the **tell** methods in the excerpt by underlining them. So that the learners can identify a rectangle:

The teacher tells the class that they will review how to identify a rectangle. First she writes "rectangle" on the board and says it has four sides. Then she tells them that a rectangle has four right angles. She asks different learners to point out a variety of right angles in the classroom. Next, she tells the class that the opposite sides of a rectangle are equal. She draws two equal lengths on the chalkboard. Then she connects these lengths with two equal widths forming four right angles. She asks the learners to write down the following steps: 1) four sides 2) four right angles 3) opposite sides equal and 4) identify a rectangle. She passes out rulers and construction paper. Then she asks the learners to draw a rectangle and cut it out. She walks around the room to correct each student's sample.

Since you will **tell** your learners what they need to know, you will want to use different **tell** methods. Remember, **tell methods deal with words, either spoken or written.** Below is a list of different teaching methods you could use to **tell**. List any other **tell** methods that you can think of:

### Tell Methods

Bulletin Board
Buzz Session
Chalkboard
Chart
Checklist
Demonstration
Discussion
Field Trip
Film
Film Loop
Filmstrip
Flannel Board
Games
Guest Speaker
Inquiry

Other

Interview
Opaque Projector
Overhead Projector
Poster
Programmed Instruction
Puppeteering
Questioning
Radio
Records
Slides
Story Telling
Tapes
Television
Testing
Textbooks
Video Tape

_____        _____

_____        _____

_____        _____

Using the list of **tell** methods on the previous page, look up any definitions of methods you don't know. Then you can **tell** yourself what they are. Ask your instructor to **show** you examples of these methods. You may want to sketch a picture of what each new **tell** method looks like. Then suggest a use for these new methods. Describe a skills content that you could deliver with each **tell** method you are unfamiliar with. Then you will be using "tell, show, do" to teach yourself.

Define: _____

_____

_____

Show

Use: _____

_____

Define: _____

_____

_____

Show

Use: _____

_____

Define: _____

_____

_____

Show

Use: _____

_____

### Showing Names, Definitions, Reasons and Steps

Another method you must use in delivering content is to **show** the learners what they want or need to learn. **Showing** is a critical source of learning. When you tell your learners that it is called "an internal combustion engine," you should also **show** them what the engine looks like. When you explain a concept like the definition of compression, you should **show** your learners a diagram of the compression cycle. Before you tell your learners about the expansion of the hot gas, you may want to **show** your learners what happens to a balloon when the gas inside is heated. Your **show** method visually explains the principle your learners need to understand the power cycle of the engine. You will also **tell** and **show** the steps of performing the skill. Then, when you **tell** the learners to check the spark plug, you **show** them how at the same time.

### LESSON PLANNING SKILLS

| Content Organization | Reviewing | ▶ | Overviewing | ▶ | Presenting | ▶ | Exercising | ▶ | Summarizing |
|---|---|---|---|---|---|---|---|---|---|
| | ⬇ | | ⬇ | | ⬇ | | ⬇ | | ⬇ |
| Content | Contingency Skill Steps | | Skill Application | | Skill Steps | | Skill Steps | | Skill Steps |
| | ⬇ | | ⬇ | | ⬇ | | ⬇ | | ⬇ |
| Methods | Telling Showing | | Telling Showing | | Telling Showing | | Telling Showing | | Telling Showing |

Some of your learners are predominantly visual. They develop a mental picture from the descriptive words you use. When you show them a picture, these learners really become involved in the learning. They see details and draw conclusions that amaze you. Your visual learners will also like to make their own pictures of what they are learning. They may even be your "day dreamers" because of the mental pictures they can conjure up so easily. While **tell** methods deal with words, **show** methods deal with pictures. The proverb "a picture is worth a thousand words" was probably coined by a visual learner.

Showing methods let your learners see what they should learn.

A picture, a diagram, a series of pictures or the action of performing the skill are what the **show** methods deliver to your learners. The most common **show** method is the demonstration. That is because the teacher does the **showing**. There are other options, however.

You may want to teach your learners how to splice an electric wire. You will, of course, **tell** them how to do it and you will also **show** them how to do it. You may ask a learner who already has the skill to demonstrate. You could use a film, slides, pictures, overhead or opaque projectors, a poster, a model, a mock-up or an exhibit to teach the skill with a series of pictures. You may use any one or several of these as **show** methods.

Some learners need to be shown what to do.

Read the following description of part of a teaching delivery. The skill that is being taught is finding the perimeter of a rectangle. This excerpt describes the second step of learning the skill: identifying and measuring the length of a rectangle. There are **tell, show** and **do** methods in the excerpt. Identify the **show** methods by underlining them.

So that the learners can learn to identify and measure the length of a rectangle:

The teacher draws a rectangle on a transparency. She tells the class the lines that are the length. She indicates these lines with green ink and writes "length." Then she measures each length with a ruler. She writes the measurement next to "length." The teacher asks the students to indicate the length of their desks. Then she asks them to measure the length of their desks. Finally, the teacher has the learners mark the length of their model rectangles with green crayons. Then the learners write down the measurement of that length. The teacher walks around the room to correct each learner's work.

Just as you want to use a variety of **tell** methods, you will want to add variety to your **show** methods. Some of the methods both **tell** and **show** your learners what they need to know. You may use them to **tell** or **show** or to do both. Remember that **show methods deal in pictures, either live or prepared.** List any other **show** methods that you can think of .

### Show Methods

Bulletin Board
Chalkboard
Chart
Demonstration
Experiments
Field Trip
Film
Film Loop
Filmstrip
Flannel Board
Games
Guest Speaker
Inquiry

Internship
Model
Mock-Up
Opaque Projector
Overhead Projector
Poster
Programmed Instruction
Slides
Story Telling
Television
Textbooks
Video Tapes

Other

_____    _____

_____    _____

_____    _____

To increase your understanding of **show** methods, define any words that you don't know from the list of the previous page. That is one way of **telling** yourself about the new method. Again, sketch a picture of what the method looks like to **show** yourself. As a **do** method, describe how you would use each new method to teach a skills content. Again, you are using "tell, show, do" to learn more efficiently.

Define:_____

_____

_____

Show

Use:_____

_____

Define:_____

_____

_____

Show

Use:_____

_____

Define:_____

_____

_____

Show

Use:_____

_____

### Do Methods Help Learners Acquire Names, Definitions, Reasons and Skills

**Tell** and **show** are methods that the teacher uses to communicate the new learning. **Do** methods are used to involve all learners in the performance of the new skill. These **do** methods are actually learning experiences the teacher plans so that the learners can participate. A laboratory which asks the learners to identify a mineral allows everyone to manipulate a mineral and the testing equipment. The learners actually perform the skill of identifying a mineral.

The teacher uses learning experiences when new words and definitions have to be learned, too. Planning activities which have the learners use these facts and concepts will involve them in writing, speaking or drawing. Keeping a list of geology definitions or diagramming a volcano are **do** methods which have the learners use the new facts and concepts they need to learn. A field trip around the school grounds can have the learners discovering eroded soil, gullies, cracked rocks or decaying plant material, which illustrate the principles of weathering and erosion. As a **do** method, you may choose to have your learners map and label the areas where these things are occurring.

## LESSON PLANNING SKILLS

| Content Organization | Reviewing | Overviewing | Presenting | Exercising | Summarizing |
|---|---|---|---|---|---|
| | ▽ | ▽ | ▽ | ▽ | ▽ |
| Content | Contingency Skill Steps | Skills Application | Skill Steps | Skill Steps | Skill Steps |
| | ▽ | ▽ | ▽ | ▽ | ▽ |
| Methods | Telling Showing Doing | Telling Showing Doing | Telling Showing Doing | Telling Showing Doing | Telling Showing Doing |

Some of your learners are kinesthetic learners. They learn by **doing**. These learners will sit back while you tell or show what is to be done . . . but not for long. After a while, they begin to fidget. As soon as they have an inkling of what the assignment is, they are ready to begin. It doesn't matter if you have not even finished giving the directions. They just want to "get busy."

"Let me do that!"
"It's my turn!"

The visual learners need to **see** how to perform the new skill. The auditory learners need to **hear** what they should do. But all of your learners need the opportunity to **do** the skill. The real learning for all of us takes place when we perform the skills we are trying to learn.

**Do** methods give your learners a chance to perform the new learning

You are providing your learners with an experience with the new skill when you have each one perform the skill. The nature of the skill will determine the **do** methods which are most appropriate. The most common **do** method is the worksheet. It provides the teacher with the opportunity to see if the learners know the right answers. Many skills cannot be performed on a worksheet because the answers only **describe** the skill. For these skills, the worksheet is not an appropriate **do** method.

You may want to teach your learners how to brush their teeth. After you have **told** them and **shown** them how to perform the skill, you will want to plan an activity for everyone to **do** the skill. That means that you will have to provide each learner with at least a toothbrush. Then you could plan role-playing, video taping, photographs, a contest or a check list. Using any one or several of these **do** methods, you provide your learners with an experience which has them practice brushing their teeth.

## Practicing Identifying Do Methods

You will want to see if you can identify the **do** methods described in the partial lesson below. Again, the skill that is being taught is finding the perimeter of a rectangle. This excerpt describes the third step of learning the skill: doubling the length of the rectangle. There are **tell**, **show** and **do** methods in the excerpt. Identify the **do** methods by underlining them.

So that the learners can learn to double the length of a rectangle:

> The teacher tells the class that "double" means to multiply by two. She writes "$2l$" on the board. Then she tells the class that double a length of 8 is 16. She writes: "$l = 8$, $2l = 16$" on the board, also.
>
> "If the length of your desk is 20 inches, what is double that length?" The teacher asks everyone to write an answer on scrap paper while she circulates around the room checking answers. Referring the students back to the rectangles they drew in the first step, the teacher asks everyone to find $2l$ of that sample. As before, the teacher circulates around the room checking the answers the learners have written.

Introducing variety into your **do** methods is essential to good teaching. Using all of your creative talents, you should expand the **do** methods that your learners will use to perform the new skills. If you select a worksheet of twenty questions to do every day, your learners won't be encouraged to practice what you want them to learn. **Do** methods involve your learners in an experience where they use the skills that are to be learned. It is not enough for your learners to **tell** or **show** you how they would do the skill.

Below is a list of **do** methods. Some of them could be used to **tell** and **show** how to do the skill, also. List any other **do** methods that you could include.

### DO METHODS

| | |
|---|---|
| Brainstorming | Model |
| Case Study | News Broadcast |
| Collection | Oral Report |
| Colloquium | Panel |
| Committees | Play |
| Contests | Practicum |
| Creative Writing | Project |
| Debate | Psychodrama |
| Exhibit | Questionnaire |
| Fair | Rating Scale |
| Forum | Research |
| Games | Role Models |
| Hands-on | Simulations |
| Improvisation | Skit |
| Inventory | Survey |
| Laboratory | Workshop |

Other

_____     _____

_____     _____

_____     _____

Just as you have learned about the **tell** and **show** methods, define any **do** methods from the list on the previous page that you are not familiar with. That is one way of **telling** yourself about the new method. Again, sketch a picture of what the method looks like to **show** yourself. To use the new **do** method, describe how you would use this **do** method when teaching a particular skill. As before, you are using **tell**, **show**, **do** to teach yourself.

Define: _____

_____

_____

Show

Use: _____

_____

Define: _____

_____

_____

Show

Use: _____

_____

Define: _____

_____

_____

Show

Use: _____

_____

Now that you have learned about the variety of **tell, show, do** methods, you will want to practice using these methods. In the pre-test assessment, you observed that an effective review lesson plan **tells** and **shows** the learners how to do the skill steps. This lesson plan will also use a method which has all the learners **do** the skill using the skill steps. Below is an example from the pre-test which shows you how to deliver the review skill step content with **tell, show, do** methods.

**Review**: Finding the main ideas

1. Teacher tells the class that the review skill is finding the main idea of reading.

2. Teacher shows the first transparency which tells the first step of the skill: (a) Read chapter once **(tell)**.

   Then shows an overlay with an example from yesterday's social studies class **(show)**. Teacher has learners read chapter in science text **(do)**.

3. Teacher continues to tell the steps **(tell)**. Gives an example of an overlay **(show)** and has the learners do the step **(do)** with the science text.
   a) Ask "What is this chapter about?"
   b) Read subtitles.
   c) Turn subtitles into a 'what' question.
   d) Find main ideas.

You are ready to apply **tell, show, do** methods to the content you teach. Begin by identifying the skill steps for the contingency skills you plan to review. You have already written these review skill steps in Chapter Two. Decide what methods you will use to **tell** the steps, **show** the steps and have the learners **do** the steps.

Skill #1
Review: _____

_____

_____

Skill #2
Review: _____

_____

_____

Skill #3
Review: _____

_____

_____

Skill #4
Review: _____

_____

_____

Skill #5
Review: _____

_____

_____

You have learned how to apply **tell, show, do** methods to the skill steps of the content. These **tell, show, do** methods are summarized below.

**T**ell.    You plan to have materials, other learners, a guest or yourself **tell** the skill steps. The telling deals with words and may be oral or written.

**S**how.    You plan to have materials, other learners, a guest or yourself **show** the skill steps. The showing uses images and may be a live demonstration or illustration.

**D**o.    You plan activities that allow all the learners to **do** the skill using the skill steps. The **doing** is an action on the part of the learners.

### Using Teaching Methods

You may feel better about writing how you would deliver the skill steps of the presentation because of all the practice exercises you have completed in this chapter. Select a new skill or the one you used in the pre-test at the beginning of this chapter and write how you would prepare the methods of the **presentation** for delivery.

_____ Skills

Skill: _____

Presentation: _____

_____

_____

_____

_____

## Discriminating Teaching Methods

The next step is a discrimination task. You are to rate the teaching methods of five different teachers. Again, only the delivery of review materials is included. Rate these portions of a lesson on a scale from 1.0 to 3.0 where 1.0 is "Very Ineffective" and 3.0 is "Minimally Effective."

1.0   Very Ineffective

2.0   Ineffective

3.0   Minimally Effective

If you feel a lesson falls between two levels on the three-point scale, you may split the gap and rate it at 1.5 or 2.5. For example, if the review seems almost effective but not quite, you would give that review a rating of 2.5. You may use a rating more than once.

**Teacher A's Lesson Plan**                    Your Rating: _____

**Review:**   How to find numbers on a number line.

1.   Teacher hangs a clothesline across the front of the room and tells the class they are going to build a number line from 0-12. Teacher passes out large numerals 0-12 and clothespins to 13 learners.

2.   Teacher asks '0' learner to tell where she or he should go on the number line. If correct the '0' can be pinned. If the learner does not know where to go, then she or he has to pass the numeral to someone who knows where the '0' goes. Continue until the number line is complete.

3.   Learners make a sketch of their own number line, 0-12, while teacher circulates around the room to correct the students' work.

**Teacher B's Lesson Plan**          Your Rating: _____

**Review:**     How to throw underhand.

1.  Teacher divides class into teams of 4 and supplies each team with a basket and 3 softballs. She then explains they are going to have a contest to see which team can throw underhand with the most accuracy.

2.  Teacher places the baskets 20 feet away from each team and explains the rules.

3.  When the learners finish, individuals compete to see which learner can throw underhand the furthest.

**Review:**    Multiply one-half times two whole numbers.

1.  Teacher writes the following steps on the chalk-board.

   a) Put whole numbers over one.

   b) Put two multiplication signs between the three numbers.

   c) Slash if possible.

   d) Multiply the three numerators for answer's numerator.

   e) Divide answer's numerator by denominator for answer.

   f) Multiply 1/2 times two whole numbers.

2.  Learners copy down steps in their notebooks.

3.  Teacher shows the learners how to do each step using the example 1/2 x 6 x 18.

**Review:**    Putting words in alphabetical order.

1. Teacher lists week's spelling words on board in random order. Teacher asks the class to explain what they would do to put words in alphabetical order.

2. Learners volunteer answers one at a time until teacher has the following steps on a flip chart:

   a) Find words that begin with 'a'.
   b) If more than one, look at second letter.
   c) If necessary, look at third letter in 'a' words.
   d) Number the order of the 'a' words.
   e) Find the words that begin with 'b'.
   f) Continue as in steps 2, 3 and 4.
   g) Alphabetize the list of words continuing through alphabet.

3. Learners take turns at chalkboard finding first, second and third words using steps. All learners complete the alphabetizing.

Your Rating: _____

**Review**:    Finding the sentence that states the story problem.

1.    Teacher unrolls a large chart which shows the following skill steps:

a) Read story.

b) Ask "What is wrong?"

c) Find the sentence that states what is wrong.

Learners take turns reading the steps from their desks.

2.    Teacher reads a short, exciting story to the learners. Then she asks, "What is wrong?"

3.    Teacher reads story once more and another learner tells what the story problem is.

You have almost finished learning how to prepare teaching methods. The ratings below will give you an idea of how well you learned what was presented. Write the difference between your ratings and the trained raters' ratings and find the sum of these differences. Divide this sum by five to determine your delivery preparation discrimination score.

| Method Preparation | Ratings | | Your Ratings | | Differences (Deviations) |
|---|---|---|---|---|---|
| A:  Number Line | 3.0 | - | _____ | = | _____ |
| B:  Throwing Underhand | 1.0 | - | _____ | = | _____ |
| C:  Multiplying | 2.0 | - | _____ | = | _____ |
| D:  Alphabetizing | 3.0 | - | _____ | = | _____ |
| E:  Story Problem | 2.0 | - | _____ | = | _____ |
| | | | Total | = | _____ |
| | | | | 5 | = _____ |

Post-Test
Teaching Methods
Discrimination
Score

If your discrimination score was more than .5, then you should go back and reread Chapter Three as well as redo the exercises. If your score was .5 or less, then you are ready to go on and learn about preparing exercises using some new methods.

There is an explanation for how the post-test ratings were determined. Teacher B's plan was rated 1.0 or "very ineffective" because she did not **tell** and **show** the skill steps. Her **do** methods were good practice if the learners already knew how to throw underhand. If the learners did not, they were only reinforcing incorrect behaviors. Teacher C's plan and E's plan received a rating of 2.0. Their delivery plans included **telling** and **showing** the review skill steps but did not include an opportunity for the learners to **do** the skill. **Tell, show, do** methods in A's and D's plans made their delivery preparations effective at 3.0.

Now you can go back and rate your own communication pre- and post-tests. To receive any score at all, your plan should include the content (i.e., a list of the skill steps). Rate your plan 1.0 if it includes just one method (**tell** or **show** or **do**). A rating of 2.0 is earned by having two of the three methods. A minimally effective plan (3.0) must include all three.

| Pre-Test Communication | Post-Test Communication |
|---|---|
| _____ Score | _____ Score |

You have learned about **tell, show, do** methods for teaching. Apply what you know about sensory input to your own learning. Multi-sensory methods can help you learn new skills more efficiently. When you set out to master a new skill, **tell** yourself about the learning. Write it, read it or tell yourself how to do the new skill. Draw it, look at pictures and diagrams and/or find visual examples of what you are trying to learn. This insures that you are using **show** methods. But the most cricital need of all is to **do** the skill you are trying to learn. Reproduce what you are trying to learn as many times, and in as many ways as you can, to insure mastery of what you want to learn. Thus you will:

1. **Tell** yourself how to do the new skill.
2. **Show** yourself how to do the new skill.
3. **Do** the new skill.

After the seminar was over, Peggy, Martha and George stuck around to catch up on each other's experiences. "That was pretty good today, huh?" remarked Martha. **"Tell, show do!** That's as easy to remember as ROPES."

"Not bad," said Peggy. "I can see where I can really use **show** methods with that third reading group. Those poor kids! They really do try to keep up. They just get so frustrated! My cooperating teacher mostly uses **do** methods with these kids . . . but the same method over and over. Those kids have dittos coming out of their ears."

"Yeah, I liked that **tell, show, do,** too," added George. "That list of methods will really help add variety to my teaching. I've been doing too much telling. That's probably why my kids are getting a little out of hand in class lately." George paused while he thought for a moment. "I really **could** use more **show** and **do** methods in my teaching."

Everyone can become a better learner with **tell, show, do** methods.

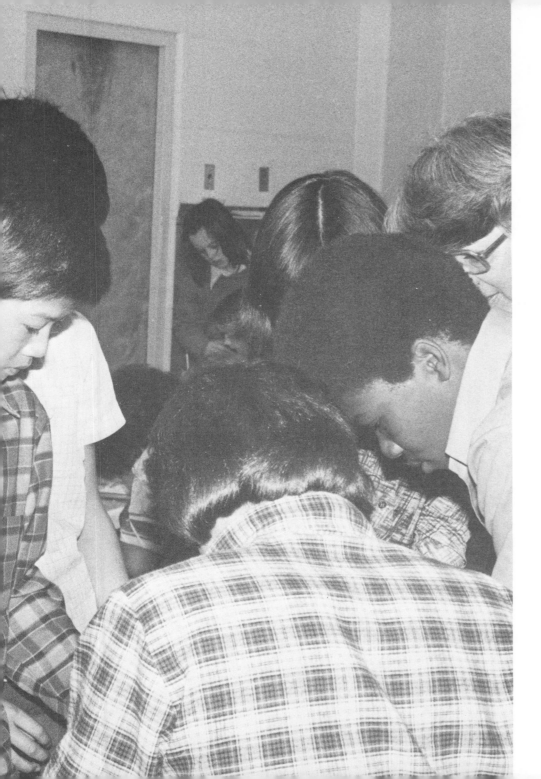

# 4

## CHAPTER 4:   PREPARING YOUR EXERCISES REPEAT-APPLY

**Experiencing Learners' Exercises**

All of you recognize the value of having the learners practice each new skill. Most of your class time is spent practicing the skill. Book companies have made millions on the workbooks, dittos and other supplemental materials they sell. Still more money is made by equipment companies who sell materials, games and equipment used to practice skills. Most teachers spend many hours each year writing supplemental practice material for the learners. And yet all of this is not enough. The effective teacher still looks for new and better ways to have the learners practice the skill.

The exercise is another opportunity to have the learners do the skill.

There are two specific ways to have the learners practice the new skill. First, the learners can **repeat** the new skill. This means that the learners only use the new skill when they practice. For example, if the learners are learning how to use a gram scale to weigh objects, that is just what they should repeat. For additional practice, the learners can apply the new skill. The learners can use the new skill in conjunction with other skills. They may weigh an object in grams (new skill) and convert the grams to ounces (old skill). This is an apply exercise because it contains more than one skill.

The learners should practice repeating just the new skill first. Once they have mastered the performance of this skill by itself, they are ready to apply the skill. When the learners perform the apply exercises, they practice not only the new skill but previously learned skills as well.

**Learning How to Get Ready**

"Peggy, this is Martha . . . Well . . . no, it's not going so good. She won't let me teach. Nothing! I've been sitting up at the back of the room now for two weeks . . . All she does is put me off. I've even offered to put up a new bulletin board and correct papers. Nothing doing . . . . Dr. Bollas? You think he'd talk to her? . . . Well listen, I'm willing to try anything! How's your little ol' third group? . . . Hey! That's great! Well at least you're teaching **some** of the time. See you tomorrow in class . . . . . Well, I haven't even got a chance to use **tell, show, do** yet . . . He said we were going to work on the presentation and the exercise . . . Yup. Well, I'm not learning how to teach, but I sure am learning how to get ready! See ya!"

Martha met with Dr. Bollas before class and told him what a difficult time she was having with her cooperating teacher. "She just won't let me do a **thing**, Dr. Bollas! " Martha concluded.

"You sound very upset, Martha, because your cooperating teacher isn't cooperating!"

"That's right, Dr. Bollas. At this rate I'll never be a teacher!" Martha was on the verge of tears.

"It makes you angry that your cooperating teacher is keeping you from becoming a teacher." Martha nodded mutely. "This is a new teacher you've got at the Campus School, Martha. Let's assume that she doesn't know when she is supposed to turn over the reins. I'll get the ball rolling with this note." He drew out a sheet of college stationery and wrote a casual note to Martha's cooperating teacher stating that he would be in at 11:00 A.M. on Tuesday to observe Martha teaching a small group of students.

"We really don't have to make a big deal out of it yet. I'm sure she just doesn't know when and how she's supposed to let you take over."

"Thanks a lot, Dr. Bollas! I really appreciate the help. And I can't tell you how much better I feel!"

"You feel relieved because you're finally going to get an opportunity to **practice** teaching, Martha. You know how important that practice is." Dr. Bollas smiled. "In fact, that's what today's seminar is about . . . practice. Let's see how good you are when it comes to your learners' practice." He handed her a pre-test and said, "You can get an early start on this."

**PRE-TRAINING ASSESSMENT OF EXERCISE PREPARA-TION SKILLS**

    Before you go further in this chapter, you will want to take a measure of how well you plan the **presentation** and **exercise** of your lesson. Select a skill and describe how you would plan to present that skill to your learners. Then write out the exercise you would give the learners to practice the skill.

Skill: _____

Presentation: _____

_____

_____

Exercise: _____

_____

_____

## Discriminating Exercises

It is difficult to explain exactly how you would plan the presentation and the exercise of a lesson. You have to teach so many different things! Perhaps it will be easier for you to discriminate how well Martha and her fellow teachers each planned a particular skill lesson. Rate their lesson plan using a five-point scale as follows:

1.0   Very Ineffective
2.0   Ineffective
3.0   Minimally Effective
4.0   Very Effective
5.0   Extremely Effective

If you feel a plan falls between two levels on the five-point scale, you may rate it as 1.5, 2.5, 3.5 or 4.5. For example, if the presentation and exercise plan seemed almost but not quite minimally effective, then you would give it a rating of 2.5.

To teach her students how to outline a chapter in their science textbooks, Teacher A first had her students read a four-page chapter. She told her learners the steps in writing an outline: first the title; next the Roman numerals; then the capital letters; the numbers; and finally the lower case letters. Teacher A had a sample outline which described how to write an outline. She placed it on the overhead. The learners took turns reading the outlined steps and then telling how they would perform that step. Finally, the learners wrote their own outlines while the teacher circulated to correct each outline.

**Teacher B's Teaching Delivery**          Your Rating: _____

Teacher B's goal was to teach his learners how to brush their teeth. He had borrowed a large model of teeth with a giant tooth brush. Very systematically, he went through the steps of tooth brushing with his learners. "First, you wet the brush and apply the toothpaste." Next, he described how to brush all the upper surfaces of the teeth; then the lower teeth. He repeated telling the steps as he showed his learners how to brush with the large model. The learners wrote the steps to brushing teeth in their notebooks. During that time, individual learners practiced demonstrating brushing the large model teeth. Teacher B gave feedback to his learners.

Today, Teacher C wanted his learners to learn how to add "ing" to words with long and short vowels. First he put "dot" and "dote" on an overhead transparency. He asked one learner to read the words and two other learners to define the words. Then he had two learners use the words in a sentence. The learners put their sentences on the chalkboard. He showed an overlay of the steps to take to add "ing" to these words. Having already diagnosed his learners as knowing long and short vowel sounds, he showed his learners how to change "cane" to "caning" and "can" to "canning." Then he had each learner add "ing" to "dot" and "dote." As a final exercise, the learners completed a worksheet giving more practice in the skill.

**Teacher D's Teaching Delivery**         Your Rating: _____

The following is a description of one of Teacher D's social studies classes. She wanted to give her children an appreciation of what it felt like to be a pioneer. First, she told her class the reasons why the pioneers left the safety of their homes for the westward trek. Then she vividly described how the journey was made to the new homesteads in the West. Reading several pages from the diary of a young girl pioneer, she had the learners think of what they would have to leave behind them if they were going to live in the wilderness. The learners took turns telling their list of things. Then she had each learner write a sentence to describe how she/he would feel leaving home. She put each child's "feeling" sentence on the new bulletin board.

Having diagnosed her learners as needing regrouping skills when subtracting two digit numbers, Teacher E wrote the following steps on the board:

1.  Start with ones column. Do you need to regroup?
2.  If no, subtract ones.
3.  If yes, regroup a ten from tens column.
4.  Subtract ones.
5.  Subtract tens.

The learners took turns reading the steps while Teacher E performed the subtraction, first with blocks and then on the board for two subtraction examples. Teacher E had groups of six learners come to the board to perform a subtraction example until everyone in the class had a chance at the board. When she had determined that they could do the skill, Teacher E had the learners do ten subtraction examples on a worksheet. As they finished, groups of four were formed to play store. Teacher E had organized different situations on slips of paper. "You have 50 cents to go to the store to buy a 20 cent candy bar. How much change should you get?" The children applied their subtraction skills with play money and grocery items.

## Checking Out Your Exercise Preparation Discrimination

Using the rating scales below, determine your pre-test discrimination score of presentation and exercise plans by obtaining the difference between your ratings and those given. Then add these differences and divide by 5.

| Exercise Plans | Ratings | Your Ratings | Difference (Deviation) |
|---|---|---|---|
| A: Outlining | 3.0 | − _____ = | _____ |
| B: Toothbrushing | 2.0 | − _____ = | _____ |
| C: Adding "ing" | 4.0 | − _____ = | _____ |
| D: Social Studies | 1.0 | − _____ = | _____ |
| E: Regrouping | 5.0 | − _____ = | _____ |
| | | Total = | _____ |

$$\frac{\qquad}{5}$$

Pre-training Exercise Preparation Discrimination Score

A satisfactory score is one of .5 or less. You may think a score of 2.0 does not seem that different. But with a five-point scale, that means that you may be rating a 3.0 lesson as "extremely effective" (5.0) or "very ineffective" (1.0). That can make a significant difference in your discrimination ability!

At this point an explanation of the ratings will serve as an introduction to the training to come. Some of the presentations and exercises seem very good and yet, according to the ratings, they were ineffective. To be minimally effective (3.0), the delivery had to include **tell, show, do** methods to teach the learners a new skill. That is, the teacher **told** the learners how to do the skill, then **showed** them how to do the skill. The learners also **did** the skill at least once. Teacher A used **tell, show, do** to score level 3.0. Teacher D (level 1.0) was extremely ineffective because she was not teaching a skill. All her creativity was channeled into **tell** methods. She could not show her learners how "to appreciate." Teacher B rated 2.0 because he did not have his learners **do** the actual skill as they would ordinarily perform brushing their teeth. Rather, he had them simulate brushing with a three-foot tooth brush, using motions that are not at all compatible with actually brushing one's teeth. Having the learners write the steps of brushing their teeth was just another **tell** method. Teacher C's 4.0 delivery was very effective because he used **tell, show, do** and **repeat** methods to teach adding "ing." The 5.0 delivery of Teacher E included all the elements of C's lesson but she added **apply** methods. Her students performed the skill with money, doing the subtraction in their heads

Now that you understand how the **tell, show, do, repeat** and **apply** scale is rated, continue reading this chapter to investigate repeat and apply methods.

"Hey, Martha," said Peggy.

Martha shook her head vigorously, "I'm not saying a word this time! I know I'm going to learn something in today's seminar. The pre-test is just helping me set my goals."

Dr. Bollas overheard the two students talking. "You're pleased that you can set goals for yourself based on the pre-test, Martha."

"Well, with a score that shows poor discriminations, I know that's one area to work on," Martha answered. "You've told us that the practice should have the learners repeat and apply the new skill. I guess I don't know what you mean by repeating and applying. So that's going to be my goal for this lesson."

"Martha is saying that she does not understand how to use repeat and apply methods. She is also stating her goal for this seminar. But there is another goal. That goal is for us to learn how to **apply** the **tell, show, do** methods to the presentation." Dr. Bollas again referred the students to a diagram on the chalkboard which showed the students what they had learned as well as the goals for today's seminar.

## LESSON PLANNING SKILLS

| Content Organization | Reviewing | Overviewing | Presenting | Exercising | Summarizing |
|---|---|---|---|---|---|
| Content | Contingency Skill Steps | Skill Applications | Skill Steps | Skill Steps | Skill Steps |
| Methods | Telling Showing Doing | Telling Showing Doing | Telling Showing Doing | Telling Showing Doing Repeating Applying | Telling Showing Doing |

"Let me add another item to your learnings about repeat and apply methods," Dr. Bollas continued. When you repeat and apply the skills you have learned, you are adding them to the **tell-show-do** methods of the exercises. These methods are really the learners' **tell-show-do**. As the learners are repeating and applying the skills, **they** are telling and showing."

Martha spoke up. "So the 'exercise' column of ROPES is really the **learners'** column. The learners tell and show as the repeat and apply.

"I'm proud of you, Martha. That's a great insight . . The exercise column represents learning in action. The exercise column is the learning outcome."

"So you **tell-show-do** everything and **repeat** and **apply** the exercises."

"Good! For our purposes right now, we will just think of the learners' **tell-show-do** the same way we think of the teachers' **tell-show-do**. In another course on learning-to-learn skills, we will focus upon learning behaviors. Right now we will emphasize the learners' repeating and applying the skills." Dr. Bollas erased the **tell-show-do** from the exercise column.

## LESSON PLANNING SKILLS

| Content Organization | Reviewing | Overviewing | Presenting | Exercising | Summarizing |
|---|---|---|---|---|---|
| Content | Contingency Skill Steps | Skill Applications | Skill Steps | Skill Steps | Skill Steps |
| Methods | Telling Showing Doing | Telling Showing Doing | Telling Showing Doing | Repeating Applying | Telling Showing Doing |

### Repetition Requires Planning

You know how important it is for the learners to **repeat** the skill. And it is necessary for them to **repeat** it more than once. It would be helpful for you to answer the following question.

"How will my learners **repeat** the skill?" In other words, what methods will you select to have the learners repeat the skill? You can use the list of methods below to find several **do** methods that the learners could use just to **repeat** the new skill. Remember that you will not want the learners to use more than one skill in the repeat exercise. Look over the list and add any other repeat methods that you can think of.

### Repeat Methods

| | |
|---|---|
| Chart | Play |
| Collection | Poster Making |
| Committees | Projects |
| Contests | Questions |
| Creative Writing | Reports |
| Debate | Research |
| Discussion | Simulations |
| Exhibit | Skit |
| Fair | Story Telling |
| Forum | Tape Making |
| Games | Transparency Making |
| Oral Report | Worksheets |
| Panel | Workshops |

Others:_____     _____

_____     _____

_____     _____

It is necessary for the learners to repeat the skill all by itself. This way they can concentrate fully on performing the skill steps of this new skill. Suppose the new skill was writing a complete sentence. Some methods that could be used for a repeat exercise are committees, contests, games, written questions and worksheets. An example of a way to plan the repeat exercise would be to have the learners form committees (method) and to answer questions (method) on a worksheet (method) using complete sentences (skill). Note that the learners are just repeating that one skill. It would not be appropriate at this time to have the learners use creative writing as a method. They would have to use other skills such as writing a topic sentence and writing a paragraph as well as the new skill of writing complete sentences.

The simplest exercise is to have the learners **repeat** doing the skill.

### Writing the Repeat Methods of a Skill

Martha scrutinized her list of **repeat** methods. "There aren't too many methods I can use to **repeat** printing 'i, l, t'," she thought. The harder she looked, the less she found. "I'd have to work pretty hard to make a game out of printing those letters. I could if I really had to. Let's see . . . a worksheet is a method I could use and the learners could work from a model. That's two! A worksheet and model seem to be the best **repeat** methods to use for this skill."

**Repeat Methods**

Skill:  Printing 'i, l, t'.

Worksheet
_____

Model
_____

### Using a Model to Select Repeat Methods

To practice selecting repeat methods, you should focus on the first skill of the five you selected in Chapter Two. Write that first skill in the space provided below. Then examine the repeat methods. Ask yourself which methods could be used to repeat this skill. Using Martha's sample as a model, write down the methods you selected to **repeat** this skill. Try to select a repeat method that will allow your students to concentrate on just the new skill.

**Repeat Methods**

Skill: ______________________________

Once you have selected the repeat methods of the exercise, consider ways that the learners can repeat the skill within these methods. It would not be sufficient practice for the learners to write one sentence or print 'i' once or add one example. You expand the repetitions within the method as carefully as you selected the method. You need to answer another question.

"How many different ways can my learners repeat the skill using the methods I have selected?"

You will write the examples or items that require the learners to repeat the new skill within the methods.

**Examining the Parts of the Skill**

To write the examples within the method, you should consider the parts that the learners will use when doing the skill. If the skill is writing a sentence, then the parts are all the words the learners know and can spell. If the skill is adding two-digit numbers to two-digit numbers, then the parts are numbers 10-99. If the skill is finding major U.S. cities on a map, then the parts are all major U.S. cities. When you know the parts that use the skill, then you can expand the ways that you have the learners repeat the skill. If you think how many words your learners know and can spell, then the number of sentences they can write for practice is almost limitless. Think how many practice examples you could write when you combine only two numbers from the ninety, two-digit numbers available to you. To list the major U.S. cities, you need only turn to the index of an atlas to give your learners plenty of repeat practice.

When you expand ways to use the skill, you are increasing your repertoire of teaching methods.

## Writing the Repeat Exercise

"The parts of my skill," mused Martha. "That's pretty easy for this printing skill. They're **i**, **l** and **t**. That is what my learners have to practice repeating." Martha continued to integrate the methods and the parts she had selected, to come up with the following repeat exercise for the skill:

### Martha's Repeat Exercise

Worksheet ▶ Name: _____ Date: _____
(Method)

Complete the following letters:

Follow the model to print 6 of each:

Model ▶
(Method)

Parts

## 150 Practicing Developing Repeat Exercises

To practice writing your **repeat** exercises, you should consider the parts of your skill. They may be defined with your skill or include things your learners know. Combine these parts with the methods you selected to write repeat exercises for your first skill.

### Repeat Exercises

Skill: _____

_____

_____

_____

Skill: _____

_____

_____

_____

Skill: _____

_____

_____

_____

Skill: _____

_____

_____

_____

**Learners Must Apply New Skills**

After the learners have performed the skill in the repeat exercise, they will need to **apply** the skill. To write the **apply** exercises, you should answer the question,"What applications should my learners use to practice the skill?"

In Chapter Two, you selected only those applications which used skills the learners had acquired. For example, Martha selected printing words and printing sentences as applications of printing 'i, l, t.' Write the applications of the first skill you selected for your learners to learn.

Applications

Skill: _____

Now that you have a list of applications for each skill, you will want to write the methods for practicing the applications. Choosing the methods used in apply exercises is accomplished in the same manner as choosing the repeat exercises. You will review the list of apply methods below with respect to the applications you just wrote. If possible, try to select different apply methods. They will add variety to the learners' practice. Take a moment now to add any other apply methods you can think of to the list below.

### Apply Methods

| | |
|---|---|
| Brainstorming | Panel |
| Case Study | Play |
| Collection | Poster Making |
| Colloquium | Practicum |
| Committees | Project |
| Contests | Psychodrama |
| Creative Writing | Questions |
| Current Events | Rating Scale |
| Debate | Reports |
| Exhibit | Research |
| Fair | Role Models |
| Forum | Simulations |
| Games | Skit |
| Hands-On Improvisation | Story Telling |
| Inventory | Survey |
| Laboratory | Worksheets |
| Model | Workshops |
| Oral Report | |

Other: _____    _____

_____    _____

_____    _____

## Understanding How to Select Apply Methods for the Exercise

A very important aspect of writing apply exercises is to be certain that the learners have already mastered all the old skills they will be expected to use within the application. This insures success with the task and mastery of the new skill. The learners will be confident of their performance and thus free to learn what you are teaching. When teaching the skill of writing a complete sentence, you could select writing a paragraph as an application if the learners have already learned how to write a paragraph. Some apply methods that could be used for applications are creative writing, current events, oral reports and story telling. To practice the skill of writing complete sentences, the learners could write a paragraph (application) on a current events topic (method) and then give a brief oral report (method) speaking in complete sentences (skill).

Applications prepare your learners to use the new learning in life situations.

As Martha examined the list of apply methods, she really thought about her applications. "If my learners were just beginning to learn how to print correctly, there aren't very many methods that I could use with my first lesson. It will be great by the fourth or fifth day when they've learned nearly all the letters. Then they can make posters and charts and stories. They'll like that! But right now they would have to practice 'i, l, t' by writing simple words and sentences. And to do that, I'm back to my modeling and worksheet method. At least for the first day."

### Apply Methods

Skill:  Printing 'i, l, t'        Application: Writing words
                                                    Writing sentences

Method:      worksheet and model

Selecting the apply methods should be a fairly easy task for you. You have already determined what application you are going to use. The next step is to match each application with an apply method. Use Martha's sample as a model to write the methods you will use to apply the first skill.

### Apply Methods

Skill: _____ Application: _____

Methods: _____

_____

Having listed the apply methods for the exercise, you should be ready to write the apply exercise. Your goal is still to have the learners perform the new skill as many times as possible. But you also want them to apply the new skill in as many different contexts as possible. To expand the applications within the method, you need to answer the following question:

"How many different ways can my learners apply the skill using the methods I have selected?"

As you write the apply exercises, you will expand the ways the learners can repeat the applications as well as the new skill.

## Examining the Parts of the Application

Just as you considered the parts of the skill to help you to expand the repeat exercises, you will identify the parts of your application to help you to expand the apply exercises. If the application is writing a paragraph, then the parts are the topic sentence, body and summary sentence. If the application is buying items costing less than a dollar, then the parts are any items that cost less than a dollar. If the application is charting large U.S. city populations, then the parts are the different kinds of charts the learners can make.

Once you know these parts, you can expand the ways the learners apply the skill. When you think about how many different topics the learners can select in current events, the number of paragraphs expands tremendously. Simulating buying two items in a candy store would easily expand the number of repetitions of the apply exercises. Consider how many different ways the learners could use a list, or pictures, or bar graphs or line graphs. When you break down all the parts of the applications, the choices increase the number of application exercises.

Expanding the applications of a skill will add variety to your teaching.

"The parts of my application are words and sentences that use 'i, l, t'. That's not difficult," thought Martha. "The learners need practice **applying** the skill to words and sentences. But there aren't many words that use only 'i, l, t'." Martha listed the words — it, lit, lilt, and tilt — and the sentences: "It lit;" and, "Tilt it." Then she combined these parts with her methods to write the following exercise:

### Apply Exercise

Skill:  Printing 'i, l, t'                    Applications:   Printing words
                                                                  and sentences

Worksheet ▶
(method)

Model ▶
(method)

Parts ◀

Name:_____ Date:_____
Write the following words 3 times each:

it _____          _____

lit _____

lilt _____

tilt _____

Write each of the following sentences 2 times each:

It lit. _____

Tilt it. _____

## 158 Practicing Apply Exercises

You need to practice writing the apply exercises for your first skill. Use the methods you selected and identify the parts of the application to write the apply exercises.

### Apply Exercise

Skill: _____ Application: _____

_____

_____

_____

_____

_____

_____

_____

_____

_____

_____

_____

_____

_____

_____

Having finished writing a repeat exercise and an apply exercise using different methods, you may want to take a look back over what you have done. The principle difference between repeat and apply exercises is that **the learners use only the new skill when they repeat. When they apply the new skill, they practice it in conjunction with previously learned skills**. Writing the exercises is accomplished by the following:

**R**epeat: Select a method that has the learners use the new skill in isolation. Then consider the parts of the skill that can be used in different combinations to increase the repetitions of the skill.

**A**pply: Choose an application that includes only those skills which your learners have already learned. Then select a method within which the application can be used for the learners' practice. Increase the number of exercises within the method by examining the different combinations possible from the parts of the application.

## 160 POST-TRAINING ASSESSMENT OF EXERCISE PREPARATION SKILLS

**Using Exercises**

Examine the principles of teaching methods you have learned.

1. **Tell** your learners how to perform the skill in words.

2. **Show** your learners how to perform the skill using images.

3. Have your learners **do** the skill.

4. Have your learners **repeat** the skill.

5. Have your learners **apply** the skill.

At the beginning of this chapter you outlined a plan for the presentation and exercise of a skill you will teach to your learners. Now you are ready to write the presentation and exercise plan again. Apply these five principles to make your planning more effective. You may use the same skill or select a different skill.

**Presentation:** _____

_____

_____

_____

**Exercise:** _____

_____

_____

_____

You now may realize that many teachers have had very little preparation for delivering effective lessons to their learners. It is not enough to use a variety of teaching methods in your delivery. You know now that an effective lesson plan will include **tell, show, do, repeat** and **apply** methods.

Study the following five teaching deliveries. Rate each teacher on a scale from 1.0 to 5.0 as follows:

1.0  Very Ineffective

2.0  Ineffective

3.0  Minimally Effective

4.0  Very Effective

5.0  Extremely Effective

If you feel a lesson falls between two levels on the five-point scale, you may rate it as 1.5, 2.5, 3.5 or 4.5.

Teacher A, a confident teacher with four years of experience, enjoyed her job in a self-contained classroom. She really got to know her twenty-eight lively children well, teaching them every day, all day.

"Today, you will learn to use rulers to measure how long things are," Teacher A said as she passed out shiny new rulers and a laboratory ditto to each learner. Directing their attention to a large cardboard model which duplicated the markings on their rulers, she asked, "What do these large markings with the numbers mean?"

"Inches! Yah, that's right! One inch, two inches . . ." Several learners in the class responded to Teacher A's question.

"That's right, Sue! Good, Tony! These marks do stand for inches," Teacher A said. Then she held up a chalkboard eraser and a ruler. She told the students the steps she was taking to measure the eraser. "First, put the end of the ruler with the 'one', at one end of what you want to measure. Then follow along the ruler until you come to the end of what you want to measure. Can you tell the class how long this is, Tom? Six inches is the right answer!"

Then Teacher A had her class use their rulers to measure the length of the lab ditto and write this figure on a piece of scrap paper. She circulated to check their answers. Dividing the class into groups of four she assigned them to different lab stations. Here the learners received additional practice measuring pre-selected items. Later in the day, Teacher A had pairs of learners measuring and cutting four-inch squares and triangles out of different colored construction paper. Then the children decorated the bulletin board with a geometric border made from their measured shapes.

Teacher B had taught in the same rural school for over seven years. She enjoyed teaching and was very systematic in the performance of her job. She never missed an opportunity to teach the children what they needed to learn. Just the other day at recess she watched a group of children playing softball. It was painful to watch them try to throw the ball to each other. Teacher B stepped in. "You children need to learn how to throw a ball before you play softball. John, Annie, Bill, Denise! Line up behind the plate." She showed the children how to hold the ball. "Hold the ball with all five fingers. They should be spread apart like this." She passed the ball to the children individually and checked the way they held the ball. "Good! Now bring the ball back behind your ear, step with the opposite foot, snap your wrist and follow through where you want the ball to go." She showed them in slow motion the steps of throwing. "Show me how you would do that." She repeated telling the steps while the children went through the motions of throwing the ball. Then each child took turns standing behind the plate and throwing the ball to Teacher B on the pitcher's mound. Teacher B watched and corrected the performance of each child. Then she had the children play a game. They could advance to first base if they could throw the ball from home plate to within a six-foot circle of first base. They took turns throwing the ball around the baseball diamond so that they could be the first to make it 'home.' Teacher B watched each throw and offered suggestions and encouragement for each throw. "You're almost home, Denise. Don't forget to step with your left leg, Bill. Good throw, John! That's the way to throw!"

Teacher C was an energetic second-year math and science teacher. His homogeneous class of average learners was composed of lively children whom he was able to control most of the time. On this bright and crisp fall day, Teacher C was prepared to teach his class how to find the area of a triangle. He had diagnosed his learners as having sound multiplication skills as well as knowing how to find the area of a rectangle. First, he told his learners that the area of a triangle was half of the base times the height. He wrote the definitions of base and height on the board. Then his learners wrote the definitions of base and height in their vocabulary lists. Teacher C then asked his learners to identify some triangles in the room.

"Over there! On the bulletin board," said Amanda. Teacher C had Amanda point out the base and height of these triangles. Then he asked for other things that were shaped like triangles.

"The sail on a boat," volunteered Josh.

"That's a triangle," Sue raised her hand and pointed to the gable of a house outside the window. "Right there where the two roofs meet. That's a triangle."

Teacher C had Josh draw a boat and Sue draw a house on the overhead projector. They outlined the triangular part of each in red. Teacher C continued to explain to his class that these triangles were really half of a rectangle. "That's why you will multiply one-half times the base times the height in your homework assignment tonight. The assignment is on the board." The children took down the assignment just as the dismissal bell rang.

Teacher D taught history. Recently, she and her class of super learners had embarked on an in-depth study of life in Colonial America. The bulletin boards were full of pictures, maps and charts depicting different facets of life in the colonies. Today, she wanted her class to investigate how the colonists obtained their clothing. First she divided the class into three groups.

"You live in the wilderness, a three days' journey to the nearest trading post," the teacher informed the first group. She pointed to the second group. "You live in a small town where you are all farmers." Teacher D told the third group that they were merchants living in Boston. Then she divided each of the three groups into pairs to answer one of the following:

What materials are your winter clothes made of?
Where did you get the material for your winter clothes?
Who made your clothes? How?

Each person in the group was to draw a sketch that illustrated the answer, as well. Using resource material, the pairs of students spent 10 minutes preparing their answers and illustrations. Teacher D circulated around the groups, giving help where needed. Then each group got up and gave their answers while the rest of the class filled in the following chart:

|  | Wilderness | Town | City |
|---|---|---|---|
| Winter Clothes Material |  |  |  |
| Where Made |  |  |  |
| Who Made and How |  |  |  |

Teacher E was a perfectionist. This was his first year of teaching in this community and he wanted to make sure that his contract would be renewed in the spring. One of his primary goals for his students was to improve their reading comprehension. He had diagnosed them as needing to be able to state the story problem.

Teacher E began his reading lesson: "When you read a story, one of the first things you want to think about is the story problem. What do I mean by 'problem,' Joey?"

Joey squirmed in his chair. "Ya mean like somethin's wrong?"

"That's right Joey. The story tells you about something that has gone wrong." Teacher E held up a picture of Little Bo Peep and asked the class what Bo Peep's problem was.

"She couldn't find her sheep," almost everyone chimed in.

Teacher E smiled and said, "Right! We just read **Charlotte's Web**. What was the main story problem in this story?" He held up the book. Some of the children raised their hands. "Estelle?"

"They wanted to kill Wilbur to eat," Estelle answered.

"That was the problem, Estelle," assured Teacher E. He took out a large poster that had: WHAT'S MY PROBLEM? written in large print and placed it in the chalk tray. "Today we will have a contest. Everyone whose birthday is in October through March over here, April through September on this side." Each child took turns answering Teacher E's questions. "My name is Hansel. What is my problem?" he asked.

"You can't find your way home," answered Joey promptly.

When they had finished, Teacher E worked with the children who were not able to answer their questions while the rest of the class worked in their spelling workbooks.

## Checking Out Your Presentation and Exercise Preparation Discriminations

Raters trained in lesson planning scored each teacher's delivery. These ratings are listed in the table below. You may determine your discrimination score by subtracting the difference between your ratings and the trained ratings. Add these five deviations and divide by 5 to obtain your discrimination score.

| Teaching Delivery | Ratings | | Your Ratings | | Difference (Deviation) |
|---|---|---|---|---|---|
| A: Measuring | 5.0 | - | _____ | = | _____ |
| B: Ball Throwing | 4.0 | - | _____ | = | _____ |
| C: Area of a Triangle | 1.0 | - | _____ | = | _____ |
| D: Colonial Life | 2.0 | - | _____ | = | _____ |
| E: Story Problem | 3.0 | - | _____ | = | _____ |
| | | | Total | = | _____ |

$$\frac{\phantom{xxx}}{5} = \underline{\phantom{xxxxx}}$$

Post-Training Exercise Preparation Discrimination Score

If your discrimination score is more than .5, you should reread Chapter 4 before continuing.

Some further feedback will help you to consolidate your learnings. Ratings of 3.0 or above mean that the teacher used **tell**, **show**, **do** methods to teach the new skill. Ratings below 3.0 mean that the teacher did not teach effectively. The highest level of teaching incorporates **tell**, **show**, **do**, **repeat** and **apply** methods. Rated at level 5.0, Teacher A's delivery of how to use a ruler to measure is the model for extremely effective teaching methods. The other teachers did not provide their learners with the opportunity of applying the new skill. Teacher C (1.0) did not **show** his learners how to find the area of a triangle nor did he give them a chance to **do** the skill in class before giving the assignment. Teacher D (2.0) employed **tell** and **show** methods, but because she was not teaching a skill, her learners could only **tell** and **show** the new facts and concepts they were learning. In order to have her learners learn a skill, she would have had to teach a skill like doing research or perhaps one of the skills of spinning or weaving. Teacher E (3.0) **told** his learners how to state the story problem. Then he **showed** them some examples. Finally, he had each child state a different story problem for his **do** method. At a level 4.0, Teacher B employed **tell**, **show**, **do** methods. Then she had her learners **repeat** the skill of throwing from home plate to first base.

At this time, you may go back and rate your communication pre- and post-training assessments. Rate your presentation and exercise plan 1.0 if it includes just one method (**tell** or **show** or **do**). A rating of 2.0 is earned from having two of the three methods. A minimally effective plan should include all three methods. Beyond a 3.0 rating, the plan can be rated 4.0 if it **tells**, **shows**, **does** and **repeats** or **applies**, and a rating of 5.0 includes all five methods.

_____ Pre-Training
Exercise
Preparation
Communication
Score

_____ Post-Training
Exercise
Preparation
Communication
Score

## Mastering Exercises

**Repeat** and **apply** methods can be applied to your own learning. When you are trying to learn a new skill, remember to repeat the skill by itself several times. For example, if you want to improve your rate of reading, you could repeat the skill by just reading quickly. You could practice repeating with a newspaper, magazine, novel, technical article, article or a textbook. When you are satisfied that you are repeating the skill correctly, then you are ready to apply the skill. You could use speed reading when doing a research paper, reading about content you will teach or taking standardized tests. Just as you will tell and show the learners how to do the skill, you will tell and show yourself how to read quickly. Next your learners will do the skill using the steps and then go on to repeat and apply the skill. In a similar manner, you will do the steps of speed reading and then repeat and apply the skill. It is exciting to understand that these methods will improve your teaching. It is even more exciting when you know how to use these methods to increase your own learning.

The exercise supports your acquisition of new learning.

". . . and next week I will begin to visit your schools to observe your teaching," concluded Dr. Bollas.

The students in the seminar looked dismayed. It wasn't that they didn't expect to be observed. After all, that's what student teaching was all about. But they were just getting into their classroom experiences. Maybe the week after next . . .?

Dr. Bollas responded to his seminar students, "You feel nervous just thinking about my first classroom observation." The students readily agreed. "The most important thing to remember for this first observation is to teach a lesson that is a skill lesson. You may be teaching the whole class or just one student. In any case, I'll be looking for the skill steps. I'll want to see you use **tell** and **show** methods to teach those skill steps. You will also make sure that your students **do** the skill. Be sure to incorporate what we learned today. Have your learners **repeat** and **apply** the skill when they practice in the exercise."

Dr. Bollas took a step toward Martha. "I know some of you may be having some problems with your cooperating teachers. Please see me about them, and together we'll try to get things straightened away before next week. See you then."

## CHAPTER 5: WRITING YOUR LESSON PLAN:
## CONTENT + METHODS

### Experiencing Planning

Years ago, lesson plans were very important for both teachers and the principal. A substitute teacher could follow these plans if the regular teacher was ill. The principal could follow the plans to monitor the regular teacher's progress through the curriculum. Some principals even went so far as to collect the plan books each week and 'correct' them when necessary. But then some changes took place.

It was easier for some teachers just to put down a page number from their text books. Planning was reduced to a series of numbers. More systematic planning was thought to stifle the creativity of the individual teacher. Spontaneity became the preferred alternative to page numbers. Now teachers and administrators are ready to look for a more effective way to plan a lesson.

It is hard to imagine Michelangelo painting the ceiling of the Sistine Chapel either by number or without planning. In fact, this incomparable level of creativity was accomplished with a great deal of artistic planning and then executed with a high level of artistic delivery skills.

We can apply Michelangelo's principles of planning and execution to classroom teaching. The teacher needs skills to both develop content and plan the lessons the learners need to learn so that she will be ready to creatively deliver these lessons.

**Lesson Planning Requires Content Organization and Method Preparation Skills**

You recognize the value of planning your lessons. Your confidence increases when you know what you are going to do next with your learners. Planning helps you to define learning goals for your learners. Further planning helps you attain these goals. To plan most effectively, you need to have planning skills. You will need content organization skills to write a lesson plan. You will also need method preparation skills for these plans.

Planning gives continuity to your teaching.

**Preparing for Lesson Planning**

The seminar students were meeting before class in the coffee shop to compare notes on Dr. Bollas's observations.

"Well, my teacher has finally let me take one of the reading groups," sighed Martha. "And my lesson didn't go too badly. Towards the end, though, you'll never guess what happened!" Martha began to giggle hysterically. "This one little kid got sick all over the place. What a mess! The class had to evacuate to the library so that was the end of my lesson. Dr. Bollas said I had done a good job with **tell, show, do** and **repeat**. I never did get to **apply**."

"My lesson wasn't that bad, thank goodness! I only had a few itchy kids who kept running to the John," joined in Peggy. "Those kids are really something, though. When you teach, you're never sure what they are going to do next."

"That's for sure," added George. "Here I thought I was doing such a great job, and Dr. Bollas just ripped me up one side and down the other about the way my class behaves." He sighed, "He says I'm too disorganized when I teach. I give the kids too much time to get into trouble. Maybe today's seminar will help. It's just that I'm teaching **everything** and I don't have time to even breathe, let alone discipline the kids."

"Better you than me, George," Martha said with a smile. "I would've quit student teaching if I was in that class. But you can handle anything, right?"

George said sarcastically, "Right, Martha. C'mon we'll be late to seminar."

Martha, George and Peggy took their seats in the seminar room. Dr. Bollas began, "From most of my observations, I can say that you are all using the teaching methods effectively. But there are still a lot of things for you to learn." Here he looked pointedly at George. "You know that! But that's why we have you practice your teaching. That's the way you will learn best."

"Today we will not take a pre-test. The pre-test that you took in the first seminar is really the pre-test for this seminar. Take a look back at that, if you have it with you, to see where you started this course." While the students looked over their original pre-tests, Dr. Bollas put the following model on the chalkboard. Then he said, "Today we are going to work on our long-range goal. That is, writing a lesson plan. First you learned how to write and organize your content using ROPES. Then you learned about **tell, show, do** methods. Last week you learned how to write student exercises using **repeat** and **apply** methods. Today you will apply those skills."

## LESSON PLANNING SKILLS

| Content Organization | Reviewing | Overviewing | Presenting | Exercising | Summarizing |
|---|---|---|---|---|---|
| Content | Contingency Skill Steps | Skill Applications | Skill Steps | Skill Steps | Skill Steps |
| Methods | Telling Showing Doing | Telling Showing Doing | Telling Showing Doing | Repeating Applying | Telling Showing Doing |

This chapter is an application of all the skills you have learned up to this point. Taking a content area, you will organize the content of that skill using the review, overview, presentation, exercise and summary structure. Then you will take that organized content and develop the **tell, show, do** methods you will use to teach the lesson. Finally, you will plan how the learners will **repeat** and **apply** the skill of each lesson. When you have completed this chapter, you should have a set of five completed lesson plans which you could use in your classroom.

## Planning the Review

**Tell, show, do, repeat** and **apply** methods are the backbone of your teaching delivery. On the other hand, review, overview, presentation, exercise and summary are the **structure** for the content you will deliver. You have to apply the content skills with the delivery skills to write a lesson plan. As a first step, consider the following question:

"What do I deliver to my learners in the review, and how do I deliver it?"

The answer is not complicated. You plan how to **tell** and **show** the steps of performing the contingency skills and you plan how the learners will **do** these skills. In other words, you **tell, show, do** the contingency skills.

Think back to Martha's exercise in Chapter Four with her handwriting skills. She planned a systematic program to teach printing using ROPES. Once she had determined **what** she was going to teach, she needed to plan **how** she would teach it.

Martha identified the contingency skills: making horizontal and vertical lines. To write her lesson plan, she planned what to **tell** and **show** her learners about making horizontal and vertical lines. She knew what to review. Then she planned how they would **do** these skills. Sometimes Martha planned to have her learners **tell** and **show** the rest of the class how to do the review skills. For the first lesson, she decided to do the telling and showing herself, using the chalkboard. Here is the first day's review that Martha planned for her teaching of printing skills.

REVIEW     **Lesson #1**

  Skill:     **Print 'i, l, t'.**     Contingency Skills:    **Making horizontal and vertical lines.**

a. Teacher shows with chalk on the board how to draw a vertical line. (Show)

b. Teacher says "Start at the top of the line. Bring your pencil down straight to the bottom line." (Tell)

c. Teacher draws a horizontal line on the board. (Show)

d. While drawing, the teacher says "Start at left where you want your line to begin. Bring your pencil straight across and stop where you want the line to end." (Tell)

e. Teacher passes out lined paper and pencils to each learner and has them reproduce patterns of lines from chalkboard. (Do)

You are ready to begin planning your week of lessons. Use Martha's review as a guide to plan the **tell, show, do** methods that will review your contingency skills. Write the review for each of the five skills you selected previously. Make sure that you **tell** and **show** each skill step and have the learners **do** the skill. Try to use different methods for each skill.

REVIEW    **Lesson #1**

Skill: _____    Contingency Skills: _____

_____

_____

_____

_____

_____

Did you **tell-show-do**?

REVIEW    **Lesson #2**

Skill: _____    Contingency Skills: _____

_____

_____

_____

_____

_____

Did you  **tell-show-do**?

REVIEW    **Lesson #3**

Skill: _____    Contingency Skills: _____

_____

_____

_____

_____

_____

Did you **tell-show-do**?

REVIEW    **Lesson #4**

Skill: _____    Contingency Skills: _____

_____

_____

_____

_____

_____

Did you **tell-show-do**?

REVIEW     **Lesson #5**

_____     Contingency Skills:     _____

_____

_____

_____

_____

_____

Did you **tell-show-do**?

## The Reviewing Tells You Where the Learners Are

When you teach the review part of your lesson, you will be especially vigilant while your learners are **doing** the skill. As you walk around the classroom and observe each learner, you can diagnose if your learners can do the contingency skills or not. The **do** method will tell you **where your learners are** in relation to both the contingency skills and the skill you plan to teach that day. For example, Martha might find that some of the learners cannot draw a straight line because they do not hold their pencils correctly. These learners need special help before they can successfully perform the contingency skills. They are not ready to learn the skills of printing.

Once you have determined that your learners can perform the contingency skills, your review is completed. Then you are ready to overview the skill.

## Planning the Overview

The next step of writing a lesson plan is to complete the **overview**. As you recall from Chapter Two, the overview teaches the learners about the uses of the new skill. That means you need to create a list of applications of the skill. Consider the following question for this, your next step of lesson planning:

"What do I deliver to my learners in the overview and how do I deliver it?"

You already know that you will deliver one or more applications of the new skill. You should plan how to **tell** and **show** the learners these applications. Then they should be able to **do** some activity which involves the application. In other words, **tell, show, do** applications of the new skill.

The review helps the learners to tie in their previous learning with the new learning.

The overview helps the learners examine what they already know about the new learning.

Next, Martha planned the **tell, show, do** methods that she would use to teach the overview of the skill. Her learners thought they knew how to print. It was her job to show them that they were lacking in the skills they needed to print legibly.

**OVERVIEW Lesson #1**

Skills:   **Print 'i, l, t'.**

a.   Before class, teacher has the learners print "The quick brown fox jumped over the lazy brown dog." (Do)

b.   Teacher corrects the sentence in red. Circle words that cannot be read. Underline letter made incorrectly. (Tell)

c.   Teacher explains to class about past messy papers. (Tell)

d.   Teacher passes back corrected sentences. (Show)

e.   Teacher explains corrections. (Tell)

f.   Teacher asks students to tell when they need to use printing. (Tell)

g.   Teacher shows some posters this year's learners and last year's learners made. (Show)

h.   Teacher asks the learners to write the numbers of the posters they would feel proud of making and why. (Tell)

i.   Teacher repeats g. and h. for learners' compositions and maps. (Show & Tell)

You are ready to write the overview for each of the five skills you are planning to teach. Using Martha's overview for a model, plan the **tell, show, do** methods you would use to teach your learners the importance of the new skills. Don't forget to use your list of applications. Again, try to select different methods for each skill.

**OVERVIEW Lesson#1**

Skill: _____

_____

_____

_____

_____

_____

_____

Did you **tell-show-do**?

**OVERVIEW Lesson#2**

Skill: _____

_____

_____

_____

_____

_____

Did you **tell-show-do?**

182

OVERVIEW **Lesson#3**

Skill: _____

Did you **tell-show-do**?

OVERVIEW **Lesson#4**

Skill: _____

Did you **tell-show-do**?

OVERVIEW Lesson#5

Skill: _____

Did you **tell-show-do**?

When you teach the overview of the lesson, you will take this opportunity to give your learners a reason for learning the new skill. It is important for the learners to see the new skill as something they need to learn. This is where your interpersonal skills come into use. You want to use applications in the overview that relate to the learners' experiences. For example, building an igloo would not be a good application to use with learners in a tropical climate. As you work to learn about the learners in your class, you will be able to select applications which are most appropriate for them. Then the learners will be ready to learn how to perform the skill, and you will be ready to teach the presentation.

## Planning the Presentation

The presentation is the third section of an effective lesson plan. In Chapter Two, you learned how to break down the skill into skill steps for the presentation. These steps are what the learners need to do in order to perform the skill correctly. In order to plan the presentation of the lesson plan, you will want to answer the following question:

"What do I deliver to my learners in the presentation, and how do I deliver it?"

What you deliver are the skill steps. The "how" of the delivery is, again, **tell, show, do**. You plan **tell** and **show** methods to deliver the skill steps to the learners. Then you plan a **do** method so that the learners can perform the skill.

The presentation gives the learners the directions they need to perform the new skill.

Martha decided that modeling was the best way of **showing** her learners how to do the steps. She planned to make the letters on lines she had drawn on the chalkboard. For **tell** methods, she planned to talk as she modeled. In addition, Martha planned a transparency which included the steps with a diagram of the step. This was another **tell** and another **show** method. Then the learners were to use pencil and lined paper to reproduce the letters — first from Martha's model and then from the transparency.

PRESENTATION    **Lesson #1**

Skill: **Print 'i, l, t'.**

a. Teacher says and shows on lines drawn on chalkboard:
   1. Start pencil on middle line 2. Make a straight line down 3. Stop at bottom line
   4. Dot over top 5. "This is an 'i'." (tell and show)

b. Teacher repeats while students follow steps on own paper. (do)

c. Teacher displays transparency (tell, show) while students repeat steps. (do)

d. Teacher says and shows on lines drawn on chalkboard:
   1. Start pencil on top line. 2. Make a straight line down. 3. Stop at bottom line.
   4. This is an 'l' (tell, show).

e. Same as b. (do)

f. Same as c. (tell, show, do)

g. Teacher says and shows on lines drawn on chalkboard:
   1. Start pencil on top line. 2. Make a straight line down. 3. Stop at bottom line.
   4. Start cross on middle line to the left of the vertical line 5. Make horizontal line stopping at right of vertical line. 6. "Print 't' (tell, show)."

h. Same as b. (do) and c. (tell, show, do)

Having already planned the review and overview of your skills, you are ready to plan the presentation. This is an important part of delivery because it is here that you teach your learners the **skill steps** of the skills. Use Martha's presentation as a model to write the **tell,show,do** methods you will use to teach the skill steps. Select from your list of methods to add variety to the lessons.

PRESENTATION: **Lesson #1**

Skill: _____

_____

_____

_____

_____

_____

Did you **tell-show-do**?

PRESENTATION: **Lesson #2**

Skill: _____

_____

_____

_____

_____

Did you **tell-show-do**?

PRESENTATION: **Lesson #3**

Skill:  _____

_____

_____

_____

_____

_____

Did you **tell-show-do**?

PRESENTATION: **Lesson #4**

Skill:  _____

_____

_____

_____

_____

_____

Did you **tell-show-do**?

PRESENTATION: **Lesson #5**

Skill: _____

_____

_____

_____

_____

_____

Did you **tell-show-do**?

**Presenting Teaches the Learners the Skill Steps**

As you teach the presentation, be especially alert for any steps you have left out. If the learners have mastered the contingency skills in the review, they should be able to use the skill steps to perform the skill successfully. While the learners are **doing** the skill steps, you should circulate around the classroom checking each learner's product. If you find more than a few learners who are unable to successfully perform the skill steps, then you should consider reteaching the presentation. When the learners have been successful in performing the new skill then they are ready for the exercise.

The exercise is the fourth section of your lesson plan. It gives the learners the opportunity to **do** the skill over and over. This repetition provides the opportunity for the learners to master the new skill. The following question needs to be answered when planning the exercise of a lesson plan:

"What do I deliver to my learners in the exercise and how do I deliver it?"

The learners need to use the skill steps as much as possible to practice performing the skill in the exercise. You need to plan methods that the learners can use to repeat the skill all by itself, as well as to apply the skill with previously learned skills. The learners will repeat and apply the new skill in the exercise.

The exercise gives the learners an opportunity to test their understanding of the skill steps.

## 190  Using a Model to Write an Exercise

As you recall, Martha's exercise had two parts: one had the learners repeat only the new skill, the other had them apply the new skill. Martha knew that her learners would need plenty of practice printing. Experience told her that the learners would need to **repeat** the skills many times to break the bad habits of doing the skills incorrectly.

EXERCISE:     **Lesson #1**

Skill:   Print 'i, l, t'

Name: _____ Date: _____

Complete the following letters:

Follow the model to print 6 of each:

*i*

l

t

Application:     **Writing words and sentences.**

Name: _____ Date: _____

Write the following words 3 times each:

**it**

**lit**

**lilt**

**tilt**

Write each of the following sentences 2 times each.

**It lit.**

**Tilt it.**

The exercise is the next part of your lesson plan to write. The learners' practice in the exercise is a critical dimension of their learning. The exercise should have the learners repeat and apply the new skill. You have already written a repeat exercise and an apply exercise in Chapter Four. You used the first of your five skills in that practice. Now complete the exercises for the remaining four skills. Use Martha's exercises as a model. Select a different **repeat** and **apply** method for each skill whenever possible.

EXERCISE:　　**Lesson #2**

Skill: _____

Application: _____

_____

_____

_____

Did you **repeat** and **apply**?

EXERCISE:　　**Lesson #3**

Skill: _____

Application: _____

_____

_____

_____

Did you **repeat** and **apply**?

192

EXERCISE: **Lesson #4**

Skill: _____

Application: _____

_____

_____

_____

Did you **repeat** and **apply**?

EXERCISE: **Lesson #5**

Skill: _____

Application: _____

_____

_____

_____

Did you **repeat** and **apply**?

**The Exercises Have the Learners Practice the New Skill**

The exercise will use most of your class time. During the exercise, you are free to circulate around the classroom checking individual learners' performances. This is a most critical stage of your teaching delivery. You are in a position to give immediate feedback to the learners on their performances of the new skill. You can diagnose the steps they may be missing. The diagnosis can reinforce the correct behaviors of the learners. They are really sure that they are performing the skill correctly.

**Planning the Summary**

The final step towards completing your lesson plan is to write the summary. The summary gives the learners another chance at doing the skill. It gives them another look at the skill steps. The following question needs to be answered when planning the summary of a lesson plan:

"What do I deliver to my learners in the summary and how do I deliver it?"

The last few minutes of class can present the learners with another look at the skill steps. Planning methods that **tell** and **show** how to do the steps once more reinforce the learning that has just taken place. In addition to **telling** and **showing** the skill steps, plan a **do** method for all the learners to repeat the skill one more time.

The summary helps the learners review the new skill one more time.

Martha looked over the three sets of skill steps which told the learners how to print 'i, l, t'. She decided that it would be appropriate to have some learners **tell** and **show** the skill steps. Because Martha had used the chalkboard in the presentation, she decided to have the learners use overhead transparencies in the summary. Using a class list on another transparency, she planned to have the learners **do** the new printing skills on the transparency next to their names.

SUMMARY:    **Lesson #1**

Skill:    Printing 'i, l, t'

a. Teacher selects a learner to print an 'i' on a transparency (show and state the steps used to write an 'i') (tell).

b. Teacher selects another learner to tell and show the 'l' and another the 't'.

c. Teacher places transparency with all learners' names down the left-hand side. Learners take turns printing 'i, l' and 't' on the transparency next to their names.

| | i | l | t |
|---|---|---|---|
| John | | | |
| Ann | | | |
| Jim | | | |
| Maria | | | |
| | | | |
| | | | |

To complete your five lesson plans, write a summary for each of the five skills. Martha's summary will serve as a model as you plan how to **tell** and **show** the·learners the skill steps once more. Then plan to have them **do** the skill again. Each summary should employ different **tell, show, do** methods.

SUMMARY:   **Lesson #1**

Skill: _____

_____

_____

_____

_____

Did you **tell-show-do**?

SUMMARY:   **Lesson #2**

Skill: _____

_____

_____

_____

_____

Did you **tell-show-do**?

196

SUMMARY:    Lesson #3

Skill: _____

_____

_____

_____

_____

Did you **tell-show-do**?

SUMMARY:    Lesson #4

Skill: _____

_____

_____

_____

_____

Did you **tell-show-do**?

SUMMARY:    **Lesson #5**

Skill:    _____

_____

_____

_____

_____

_____

Did you **tell-show-do**?

When teaching the summary, you have one more chance to reteach the new skill to the learners. The learners may now understand enough about the new skill to ask questions they need answered: "Why did the paper turn pink?" "Why do you do the opposite?" "Why does it do that?" The more exposure your learners have to the new skill, the more they will be able to diagnose their own learning. The summary can bring the learners one step closer to real understanding.

## Using ROPES Content Methods to Write a Lesson Plan

Having completed a set of five lesson plans, you may want to look back to summarize what you have learned. The major divisions of your lesson plans are **review, overview, presentation, exercise** and **summary**. The content of the lesson plan reviews the skill steps of any contingency skills, and overviews any relevant applications of the new skill. The presentation of the skill steps, exercises for the skill, as well as the summary of the skill steps, complete the content of the lesson plan.

### LESSON PLAN MODEL

| Content Organization | Reviewing | Overviewing | Presenting | Exercising | Summarizing |
|---|---|---|---|---|---|
| Content | Contingency Skill Steps | Skill Applications | Skill Steps | Skill Steps | Skill Steps |

**Using Tell-Show-Do-Repeat-Apply Methods to Write a Lesson Plan**

Once the content has been organized, you may determine the methods that will be used to teach the learners. Every time you teach skill steps, you will use **tell, show, do** methods. That means you **tell, show, do** the review, presentation and summary. The overview gives a broader picture of the skill and its applications. **Tell, show, do** these applications in the overview. The exercise has the learners use **repeat** and **apply** methods to practice the new skill. Use these content organization and teaching methods skills to develop your lesson plan on the post-test.

## LESSON PLAN MODEL

| Content Organization | Reviewing ▶ | Overviewing ▶ | Presenting ▶ | Exercising ▶ | Summarizing |
|---|---|---|---|---|---|
| Content | Contingency Skill Steps | Skill Applications | Skill Steps | Skill Steps | Skill Steps |
| Methods | Telling Showing Doing | Telling Showing Doing | Telling Showing Doing | Repeating Applying | Telling Showing Doing |

# POST-TRAINING ASSESSMENT OF LESSON PLANNING

## Using Communication Lesson Planning Skills

It will seem much easier to write a lesson plan now that you have just completed writing 5 different plans. You have been told how to write a lesson plan; you have been shown how to write a lesson plan; and, you have practiced it. With this increased confidence in your ability, select a new skill or the one you used in the pre-test at the beginning of this book. Write a lesson plan for the review, overview, presentation, exercise and summary of this skill.

Post-Training Lesson Plan

Skill: _____

As you have come to expect, the next task will measure your ability to discriminate effective lesson planning. Rate these lessons on a scale from 1.0 to 5.0 where 1.0 is "Very Ineffective" and 5.0 is "Extremely Effective."

1.0  Very Ineffective

2.0  Ineffective

3.0  Minimally Effective

4.0  Very Effective

5.0  Extremely Effective

If you feel a lesson falls between two levels on the five-point scale, you may rate it as 1.5, 2.5, 3.5 or 4.5. For example, if the plan seems almost "extremely effective" but not quite, you would give that lesson a rating of 4.5. You may use a rating more than once.

**Lesson Plan A: Using a Ruler**          Your Rating: ——————————

1.  To review how to find numbers on a number line, the teacher hangs a clothesline across the front of the room and tells the class they are going to build a number line from 0-12. Teacher passes out large numerals 0-12 and clothespins to 13 learners.

2.  Teacher asks '0' learner to tell where she or he should go on the number line. If correct, the '0' can be pinned. If the learner does not know where to go, then she or he has to pass the numeral to someone who knows where the '0' goes. Continue to complete the number line.

3.  Learners make a sketch of their own number line, 0-12, while teacher circulates to correct.

4.  Then the teacher will have each learner take a turn at the chalkboard to draw a 'straight' line and sign their names.

5.  Select any learners that pick up the yardstick to draw the line. Ask the learners to select which lines are the straightest.

6.  Then have learners tell how they would measure the lines they drew. Teacher tells and shows the applications of using a ruler to measure and draw straight lines.

7.  Teacher uses a large cardboard model of a ruler and passes out rulers and laboratory dittos to each learner. She uses question-and-answer to write the following steps on the board: a) The large marks stand for inches; b) put the end of the ruler with one inch at one end of what you are measuring; c) follow along the ruler to the right until you come to the end of what you want to measure.

8.  Teacher shows the class how to follow the steps using an eraser from the chalkboard. Then the learners measure their lab sheets and write down their answers while the teacher circulates around the room.

9.  Learners do lab sheets in groups of four to measure pre-selected items. Then groups of two measure and cut four inch squares and triangles out of construction paper to decorate bulletin board with geometric border.

10. Teacher reviews the skills steps of measuring by having one learner write the steps on a transparency and another show the steps. Then learners measure their feet and record the length on the chalkboard.

1.   Teacher reviews how to throw underhand by modeling the throw while she tells the steps: a), Hold ball with fingers spread and palm up; b), bring arm back to throw while other arm is forward; c), step with opposite foot as arm comes forward; d), follow-through where you want the ball to go, palm up.

2.   Each learner takes 3 turns throwing underhand into a basket 20 feet away.

3.   Teacher shows a short film clip that shows the field work in a softball game. She wants the learners to pay particular attention to the players' throwing.

4.   Learners write down 3 things they observed the players doing when they threw accurately.

5.   Learners discuss their lists of observations with the rest of the class while the teacher relates the principles of throwing from the examples; i.e., stepping into the ball made it travel quickly.

6.   Teacher shows the learners how to throw overhand while telling them the steps to throwing: a), Hold the ball with all five fingers, spread apart like this; b), bring the ball back behind your ear like this; c), step with the opposite foot; d), snap your wrist and follow through where you want the ball to go.

7.   Children line up and practice throwing in slow motion as teacher tells the steps one more time.

8.   Children play a game which has them practice throwing from home plate to first base, to second base, to third base and then home.

9.   After game, teacher shows the learners one more time how to throw overhand with several students doing the modeling as the teacher tells the steps.

10.   Students take 3 turns throwing the ball into baskets.

**Lesson Plan C: Finding Information For a Research Paper**     **Your Rating:**———————

1. To review alphabetical order, the teacher lists week's spelling words on board in random order. Teacher asks the class to explain what they would do to put the words in alphabetical order.

2. Learners volunteer answers one at a time until teacher has the following steps on a flip chart: a), Find words that begin with 'a'; b), if more than one, look at second letter; c), if necessary, look at third letter; d), number the order of 'a' words; e), find the words that begin with 'b'; f), continue as in steps 2, 3 and 4; g), alphabetize a list of words continuing through alphabet.

3. Teacher shows class different sketches drawn from the Colonial Period which portray the dress of different kinds of people.

4. Teacher explains that today the students are going to try to answer the following questions depending on what group they are assigned to:

    "What materials are your winter clothes made of?"
    "Where did you get the material for your winter clothes?"
    "Who made your clothes? How?"

5. Teacher assigns students to groups of two: some groups are farmers living in a small town; other groups are pioneers living in the wilderness, a three days' journey to the nearest trading post; and the third set of groups are merchants living in Boston.

6. Using assigned resource material, pairs of students spend 20 minutes preparing their answers and illustrations (by drawing sketches of the costumes).

7. Teacher circulates around the room giving help where needed.

8. Each group gets up and gives their answers while the rest of the class fills in the following chart:

|  | Wilderness | Town | City |
|---|---|---|---|
| Winter Material |  |  |  |
| Where Made |  |  |  |
| Who Made |  |  |  |

1. To review how to multiply 1/2 times two whole numbers, the teacher writes the following steps on the chalkboard: a), Put whole number over one; b), put two multiplication signs between the three numbers; c), slash if possible; d), multiply the three numerators for answer's numerator; e), divide answer numerator by the product of the denominator; f), get answer to 1/2 times two whole numbers.

2. Learners copy down steps in their notebooks.

3. Teacher has the learners identify some triangles in the room.

4. Students then draw their examples on an overhead transparency, outlining the triangular parts in red.

5. Teacher shows that a triangle is really half a rectangle. He does this by cutting a piece of construction paper in half along the diagonal.

6. Teacher uses the overhead to tell how other kinds of triangles are really half a rectangle.

7. Learners take notes on the different kinds of triangles.

8. Teacher writes the formula for finding the area of a triangle on the board: A - 1/2 b h.

9. Learners outline a sample triangle to show the base and the height.

1.  Teacher reviews finding the sentence that states the story problem, by unrolling a large chart which shows the following skill steps: a), Read story; b), ask "What is wrong;" c), find the sentence that states what is wrong. Learners take turns reading the steps from their desks.

2.  Teacher reads a short, exciting story to the learners. Then she asks "What is wrong?"

3.  Teacher reads story once more and learners raise hands when they hear the sentence that is the story problem.

4.  Learners write down a problem they may have. Teacher asks the learners to write several sentences about their problem and how they solved that problem.

5.  Teacher tells the learners that problems and solutions make good stories. When they can find the story problem, they will be looking for how the problem got solved.

6.  Teacher adds two more steps to the review chart: d), read the sentence that states the story problem again; e), write the basic meaning of that sentence in your own words.

7.  Teacher asks about reading the class has done together. "What was the main story problem in **Charlotte's Web**?" Teacher follows the steps, asking the students to answer each step.

8.  Teacher shows large poster — "What's My Problem?" — and divides class in half to play a game. Each child has turn answering a question: i.e., "My name is Hansel. What is my problem?"

9.  Teacher summarizes what the students have learned by pointing out the steps again and giving an example from a two paragraph worksheet that the students have. The learners state the story problem of the second paragraph on their own.

As you approach the end of learning how to write a lesson plan, you may be eager to see how much you have learned. The ratings below will give you an idea of how much you have increased your ability to discriminate effective lesson planning. Write the difference between your ratings and the given ratings and find the sum of these differences. Divide this sum by five to determine your lesson planning discrimination score.

| Lesson Plans | | Ratings | | Your Ratings | | Difference (Deviation) |
|---|---|---|---|---|---|---|
| A: | Using a Ruler | 5.0 | - | _____ | = | _____ |
| B: | Ball Throwing | 4.0 | - | _____ | = | _____ |
| C: | Researching | 2.0 | - | _____ | = | _____ |
| D: | Geometry | 1.0 | - | _____ | = | _____ |
| E: | Stating the Problem | 3.0 | - | _____ | = | _____ |
| | | | Total | = | | _____ |

$$\frac{}{5} = \underline{\qquad}$$

Post-Training
Lesson Planning
Discrimination
Score

If your discrimination score was more than .5, you should go back and reread Chapter Five as well as redo the exercises. If your score was .5 or less, then you are ready to go on and finish the text.

As a summary of what you have learned about lesson planning, read the following explanation of the post-test ratings. The geometry plan was rated 1.0 or "extremely ineffective" because it used only one method, **tell**. The learners were not **shown** how to find the area of the triangle nor did they **do** the skill. The research plan was rated a 2.0 or "ineffective," because it included only **tell** and **show** methods. It did not have the learners **do** the skill. At a "minimally effective" level of 3.0, the story problem lesson plan included **tell, show, do** methods for the review, overview, presentation and summary. This was also true for the throwing (4.0) and the ruler (5.0) plans. However, the latter two both included an exercise which had the learners **repeat** the skills. The ruler plan was rated "extremely effective" because the exercise included **applications** of the skill of measuring which had the students create a geometric decorative border.

At this time, you can go back and rate your communication pre- and post-tests. The appropriate pre-test, of course, is the one which you completed in Chapter One. To receive any score at all, your plan must include the content of the review, overview, presentation, exercise and summary. Rate your plan 1.0 if it includes just one method (**tell** or **show** or **do**). A rating of 2.0 is earned from having two of the three methods. A minimally effective plan should include all three methods. Beyond a 3.0 rating, the plan can be rated 4.0 if it **tells, shows, does** and **repeats** or **applies**. A rating of 5.0 includes all five methods.

_____ Pre-Training          _____ Pre-Training
                                 Lesson Planning                                        Lesson Planning
                                 Score (from                                            Score (from
                                 Chapter One)                                           Chapter Five)

"I'd like to see you for a few minutes, George," said Dr. Bollas at the end of class. As the rest of the students left the room, Dr. Bollas offered George a chair beside his desk. "I've been thinking about your problems, George."

"I've been doing a lot of thinking, too," responded George. "I really want to make a go of my teaching."

"You're concerned because you want to do a good job but you're not really sure how."

"Well . . . it isn't that I don't know how so much as that I'm just plain overloaded."

"You're saying that you have too many responsibilities with the class to handle any one with expertise."

"That's just it! If I could ever get organized!"

"What about today's class? How did you do on the post-test?"

George looked over his test results, "Well, I got a 3.0 on my lesson plans. I forgot to have the kids repeat the skill in the exercise. And I got a .4 in the discrimination test."

"That must make you feel pretty good to be able to do so well with a new set of skills. And that is where we are going to start. As I see it, you've basically got two courses of action: To use your lesson planning skills to get organized, or, to drop back to teach only a small group. What's it going to be, George?"

George replied without hesitation "The first one. I don't like to quit, and the second course of action sounds like quitting to me. After all, I'm going to have to teach the whole class day after day when I'm a teacher! I think I can go ahead and write some decent lesson plans. That way I'll be able to keep my class busy learning!"

# 6

## CHAPTER 6: SUMMARY

### DEVELOPING YOUR TEACHING DELIVERY

#### Preparing for Teaching

There are so many things for you to do when you teach! Preparing your lesson plans will take much time. But you want to do all that you can to teach your learners effectively. You will feel more confident when you get up to teach knowing you have planned what you are going to do. And the learners will be able to learn more efficiently when they are systematically taught the skills they need to learn. Lesson planning is just **one** of the many skills that effective teachers need and use.

With effective teaching, your learners will grow.

Preparation for teaching begins with identifying what the learners need to learn by developing your content. Next, you will plan how to **diagnose** your learners so that you can respond to the learners in the teaching delivery. This will allow the learners to begin the first phase of learning — **exploring** what they know. You plan to **set the goals** the learners need so that you can personalize the teaching delivery for them. Then the learners will **understand** what they do not know. Finally, you **plan your lessons** so that you can initiate your delivery with your learners. Thus, the learners can **act** to learn what they need to learn — the final phase of learning.

**PHASES OF TEACHING AND LEARNING**

|  |  |  | I | II | III |
|---|---|---|---|---|---|
| Teacher: | Teaching Preparation Skills | Developing ▶ Content | Diagnosing | Setting Goals | Planning Lessons |
|  |  |  | ⇨ ↗ | ⇨ ↗ | ⇨ |
| Learner: | Learning Skills |  | Exploring | Understanding | Acting |

Planning your lesson is really an early stage of making your teaching delivery. Used in conjunction with interpersonal and other teaching preparation skills, lesson planning supports the teaching delivery. The teacher uses her interpersonal skills to **attend** and **respond** to the learners' frames of reference, **personalize** the learning goals and **initiate** steps to achieve those goals. The teacher uses her lesson planning skills to develop the lessons necessary to deliver skills to the learners. Now, in making her teaching delivery, the teacher uses both teaching preparation and interpersonal skills concurrently. She uses her content development skills to develop her content, her diagnostic skills to diagnose the learners in terms of the content, her goal setting skills to set learning goals based upon the diagnosis. Finally, she uses the product of her lesson planning skills when implementing the lesson plan: by using **ROPES** to organize the delivery of her content and by **telling-showing-doing** every phase of **ROPES,** and **repeating** and **applying** the **exercise phase.** At the same time, she uses her interpersonal skills to make the direct delivery to the learners: attending to the learners as she develops her content; responding to the learners' experiences as she diagnoses their levels of functioning with the content; personalizing their experience in terms of setting goals; initiating with them by implementing the lesson plan to deliver the skills they need.

## PHASES OF TEACHING AND LEARNING

|  |  |  | I | II | III |
|---|---|---|---|---|---|
| Teacher: | Teaching Preparation Skills | Developing Content **+** | Diagnosing **+** | Setting Goals **+** | Planning Lessons **+** |
|  | Interpersonal Skills | Attending ▶ | Responding | Personalizing | Initiating |
| Learner: | Learning Skills |  | Exploring | Understanding | Acting |

When you plan your lessons, you begin by identifying the contingency skills your learners need to **review**. Then you decide on the **tell, show, do** methods you will use to reteach the contingency skill steps. The learners will be able to hear, see and do the first part of the lesson. In all probability, your learners will already know how to do the contingency skills. But you want the learners to have success early in the lesson. They will feel more confident as they explore what they know. You may hear them say:

"We can do that!"

"We learned that last week!"

"What a cinch!"

## LESSON PLANNING SKILLS

Content
Organization                    Reviewing
                                   ▽

Content                         Contingency
                                Skill Steps
                                   ▽

Methods                         Telling
                                Showing
                                Doing

## Overviewing So That the Learners Know When to Use the Skill

The second part of your lesson should **overview** the applications of the new skill. You want the learners to know when to use the skill. The overview also previews what the skill looks like. Again, you will plan the **tell, show, do** methods that will be used to overview the skill. These methods will give the learners an opportunity to explore if they know when to use the skill, or, if they even recognize the skill. And as the learners explore in the overview, they may say:

"So that's what a thermometer is!"

"I've seen one of those before."

"Oh! That's what we're going to learn to use today!"

### LESSON PLANNING SKILLS

| Content Organization | Reviewing ▶ | Overviewing |
|---|---|---|
| | ▽ | ▽ |
| Content | Contingency Skill Steps | Skill Applications |
| | ▽ | ▽ |
| Methods | Telling Showing Doing | Telling Showing Doing |

The **presentation** is the "meat" of the lesson you plan to teach. After deciding on the methods to use, you will **tell, show, do** the skill steps. During the presentation, the students will learn how to do the skill. They will use their ears and eyes to examine the skill steps. Then they will try **doing** the skill themselves, following the skill steps. The systematic presentation will give them needed direction. And as they understand what to do, you may hear them say:

"So that's how you do that!"

"I think I can do that!"

"That doesn't look too hard!"

### LESSON PLANNING SKILLS

| Content Organization | Reviewing ▶ | Overviewing ▶ | Presenting |
|---|---|---|---|
| | ⬇ | ⬇ | ⬇ |
| Content | Contingency Skill Steps | Skill Applications | Skill Steps |
| | ⬇ | ⬇ | ⬇ |
| Methods | Telling Showing Doing | Telling Showing Doing | Telling Showing Doing |

If the presentation is the "meat" of the lesson, the exercise is the "gravy." Your learners need to be involved in the learning to maximize their success with the new skill. First you will plan methods that have the learners **repeat** the new skill. As the learners **repeat** the skill, they will be involved in the action phase of learning. When they know how to do the skill, you will want the learners to practice **applying** the skill. As they use the new skill in conjunction with previously learned skills, the learners will be prepared to recycle their learning. They will explore, understand and act in relation to the application exercises as they say:

"Hey! Look at that!"

"That's really neat the way that worked."

"I know where I can use that!"

## LESSON PLANNING SKILLS

| Content Organization | Reviewing ▶ | Overviewing ▶ | Presenting ▶ | Exercising |
|---|---|---|---|---|
| | ▽ | ▽ | ▽ | ▽ |
| Content | Contengency Skill Steps | Skill Applications | Skill Steps | Skill Steps |
| | ▽ | ▽ | ▽ | ▽ |
| Methods | Telling Showing Doing | Telling Showing Doing | Telling Showing Doing | Repeating Applying |

The last phase of your lesson is the **summary**. The summary gives you another opportunity to reteach the skill steps to the learners. While the learners may have understood some aspects of performing the new skill, the summary repeats the teaching. You will plan the **tell, show, do** methods that you will use to teach the summary. Then your learners will have another chance to explore, understand and act in relation to the new skill. They may say:

"Oh! Now I understand why we did that!"

"Maybe I can do this over here!"

"I've really got it this time!"

## LESSON PLANNING SKILLS

| Content Organization | Reviewing | Overviewing | Presenting | Exercising | Summarizing |
|---|---|---|---|---|---|
| Content | Contingency Skill Steps | Skill Applications | Skill Steps | Skill Steps | Skill Steps |
| Methods | Telling Showing Doing | Telling Showing Doing | Telling Showing Doing | Repeating Applying | Telling Showing Doing |

In preparing for teaching and in relating interpersonally to the learners, the teacher herself is recycling exploration, understanding and action. It simply makes good sense that the teacher learns just as her learners do. She **explores** where she is in relation to the learners in order to **understand** where she wants or needs to be; she **acts** to get from where she is to where she wants to be. She **E-U-A**'s within both the teaching preparation skills and the interpersonal skills. That is to say, in the absence of the learners, the teacher explores, understands and acts to prepare for the learners. In the presence of the learners, the teacher **E-U-A**'s to make a delivery to the learners. In a very real sense, the teacher **E-U-A**'s every teaching behavior that she directs toward the learners. In this way, she insures the most extensive exploration, the most accurate understanding and the most effective action that she needs to reach and deliver to the learners.

### PHASES OF LEARNING

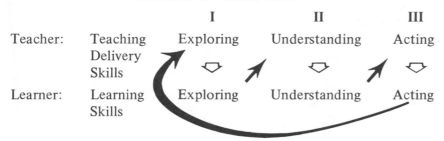

|          |                               | I          | II            | III      |
|----------|-------------------------------|------------|---------------|----------|
| Teacher: | Teaching Delivery Skills      | Exploring  | Understanding | Acting   |
| Learner: | Learning Skills               | Exploring  | Understanding | Acting   |

The "end" of teaching is learning. The "means" of teaching is learning as well. The teacher must herself be engaged in a continuous learning process so that she can make a learning delivery to the learner. At each stage of her delivery, she is guided by the effectiveness of the learners' involvement in **E-U-A**. That is, as the teacher **E-U-A**'s each teacher behavior, so does the learner ultimately **E-U-A** each learner behavior. Indeed, the ultimate purpose of teaching is to transform learners into teachers. That transformation is seen most clearly during the exercises when the learners **tell** and **show** the **repeat** and **apply** exercises  which  they are **doing**. The ultimate purpose of teaching is to involve the learners in a life-long learning process — just as the teacher is involved.

### PHASES OF LEARNING

| | | I | II | III |
|---|---|---|---|---|
| Learner: | Learning Skills | **Exploring** ▶ What you know | **Understanding** ▶ What you need to know | **Acting** To learn what you need to learn |

The semester ended with mixed emotions on the part of the student teachers. They were glad to be coming back to the campus to be with all their friends again. They had missed the interactions with their fellow students. But now they knew they would miss their own learners. They had made a difference to these kids. And the children had helped the student teachers grow. For the first time, many of the student teachers had to put someone else first. They had learned to work hard planning lessons that would teach their learners what they needed. They had learned to respect the teaching skills necessary to do the job right.

Some of them had been given farewell parties, many of them punctuated by tears. Others had received little grubby gifts that their students had made to remember them by — and here and there a passionate note of love and admiration when the student teacher had really touched some child's soul. Yes, this was all hard to leave behind.

Peggy, Martha and George had finished their practice teaching strongly. They had used every teaching skill Dr. Bollas taught them in seminar. Peggy graduated from the third reading group to the top reading group. She knew that her cooperating teacher must have approved of her teaching by trusting her with the top students. George finally got on top of his teaching, too. Dr. Bollas jokingly referred to him as the "most improved player of the season." George had stuck with all his responsibilities and worked hard. And it had paid off. The principal of the North School had offered George a job for next year.

Martha got her chance to teach. And somehow, all those years of school began to pay off. Dr. Bollas recognized her as a 'natural.' She was one of those rare people who make superb teachers. Her enthusiasm captured her students. They learned in spite of themselves. The only problem Martha had was with her jealous cooperating teacher.

Martha felt confident about her chosen career. She was happy as she prepared to take part in what all experienced teachers know to be the second greatest privilege: helping others to learn.

# BIBLIOGRAPHY

Aspy, D.N.
**Toward a Technology for Humanizing Education**
Champaign, Illinois: Research Press, 1972
Useful for understanding the research base for the facilitative interpersonal dimensions of the Carkhuff Model in education. Contains introductions to Flanders Interaction Analysis and Bloom's cognitive processes as well as empathy, congruence and regard. Concludes that teachers with high levels of interpersonal skills have students who achieve more.

Aspy, D.N. and Roebuck, F.N.
**Kids Don't Learn from People They Don't Like**
Amherst, Massachusetts: Human Resource Development Press, 1977.
Useful for understanding the research base for the Carkhuff Model in teaching. Studies the differential effects of training in Flanders, Bloom and Carkhuff skills. Hundreds of teachers were trained. The effects on thousands of learners were studied. Significant gains were achieved on the following indices: student absenteeism and tardiness; student discipline and school crises; student learning skills and cognitive growth. Concludes that the Carkhuff model is the preferred teacher training model.

Berenson, B.G.
**Belly-to-Belly and Back-to-Back: The Militant Humanism of Robert R. Carkhuff**
Amherst, Massachusetts: Human Resource Development Press, 1975.
Useful for an understanding of the human assumptions underlying the human and educational resource development models of Carkhuff. Presents a collection of prose and poetry by Carkhuff. Concludes by challenging us to die growing.

Berenson, B.G. and Carkhuff, R.R.
**The Sources of Gain in Counseling and Psychotherapy**
New York: Holt, Rinehart and Winston, 1967.
Useful for an in-depth view of the different orientations to helping. Integrates the research of diverse approaches to helping. Concludes with a model of core conditions around which the different preferred modes of treatment make their own unique contributions to helpee benefits.

Berenson, B.G. and Mitchell, K.M.
**Confrontation: For Better or Worse**
Amherst, Massachusetts: Human Resource Development Press, 1974.
Useful for an in-depth view of confrontation and immediacy as well as the core interpersonal dimensions. Presents extensive experimental manipulation of core interpersonal skills and confrontation and immediacy. Concludes that while confrontation is never necessary and never sufficient, in the hands of an effective helper, it may be efficient for moving the helpee toward constructive gain or change.

Berenson, D.H., S.R. Berenson and Carkhuff, R.R.
**The Skills of Teaching— Content Development Skills**
Amherst, Massachusetts: Human Resource Development Press, in press, 1977.
Useful for learning skills needed for developing teaching content. Develops skills based content in terms of do and think steps and supportive knowledge in terms of facts, concepts and principles. Concludes that content must be developed programmatically in order to insure teaching delivery.

Berenson, S.R.; Carkhuff, R.R.; Berenson, D.H. and Pierce, R.M.
**The Do's and Don'ts of Teaching**
Amherst, Massachusetts: Human Resource Development Press, 1977.

Useful for pre-service and in-service teachers. Lays out the interpersonal skills of teaching and their effect in the most basic form. Concludes that effective teachers apply skills that facilitate their learners' involvement in learning.

Carkhuff, R.R.
**Helping and Human Relations.**
**Vol. 1. Selection and Training**
**Vol. 2. Practice and Research**
New York: Holt, Rinehart and Winston, 1969.

Useful for understanding the research base for interpersonal skills in counseling and education. Operationalizes the helping process in great detail. Presents extensive research evidence for systematic selection, training and treatment procedures. Concludes that teaching is the preferred mode of treatment for helping.

Carkhuff, R.R.
**The Development of Human Resources:**
**Education, Psychology and Social Change**
New York: Holt, Rinehart and Winston, 1971.

Useful for understanding applications of human resource development (HRD) models. Describes and presents research evidence for numerous applications in helping skills training in human, educational and community resource development. Concludes that systematic planning for human delivery systems can be effectively translated into human benefits.

Carkhuff, R.R.
**The Art of Helping III**
Amherst, Massachusetts: Human Resource Development Press, 3rd Edition, 1977

Useful for learning helping skills. Includes attending, responding, personalizing and initiating modules. Concludes that helping is a way of life.

Carkhuff, R.R. and Berenson, B.G.
**Beyond Counseling and Therapy**
New York: Holt, Rinehart and Winston, 2nd Edition, 1977.

Useful for understanding of the core interpersonal conditions and their implications and applications. Adds many core dimensions and factors them out as responsive and initiative dimensions. Includes an analysis of the client-centered, existential, psychoanalytic, trait-and-factor and behavioristic orientations to helping. Concludes that only the trait-and-factor and behavioristic positions make unique contributions to human benefits over and above the core conditions.

Carkhuff, R.R. and Berenson, B.G.
**Teaching As Treatment**
Amherst, Massachusetts: Human Resource Development Press, 1976.

Useful for understanding the development of a human technology. Operationalizes the helping process as teaching. Offers research evidence for living, learning and working skills development and physical, emotional and intellectual outcomes. Concludes that learning-to-learn is the fundamental model for living, learning and working.

Carkhuff, R.R.; Berenson, D.H. and Berenson, S.R.
**The Skills of Teaching—Lesson Planning Skills**
Amherst, Massachusetts: Human Resource Development Press, in press, 1977.

Useful for learning skills needed to prepare for delivering content. Organizes lessons by reviewing, overviewing, presenting, exercising and summarizing. Breaks the organization down into a tell-show-do format. Concludes that content must be delivered in programmatic ways in order to maximize learning.

Carkhuff, R.R.; Devine, J.; Berenson, B.G.; Griffin, A.H.; Angelone, R.; Keeling, T.; Patch, W. and Steinberg, H.
**Cry Twice!**
Amherst, Massachusetts: Human Resource Development Press, 1973.

Useful for understanding the ingredients of institutional change. Details the people, programs and organizational variables needed to transform an institution from a custodial to a treatment orientation. Concludes that institutional change begins with people change.

Carkhuff, R.R and Pierce, R.M.
**Teacher As Person**
Washington, D.C.: National Education Association, 1976.

Useful for teachers interested in ameliorating the effects of sexism and racism. Includes modules and applications of interpersonal skills in the school. Concludes that behaviors teachers practice influence learning students accomplish.

Rogers, C.R.; Gendlin, E.T.; Kiesler, D. and Truax, C.B.
**The Therapeutic Relationship and Its Impact**
Madison, Wisconsin: University of Wisconsin Press, 1967.

Useful for understanding the transitional phases in developing HRD models. Presents extensive evidence on training lay and professional helpers as well as different orientations to helping. Concludes that the core interpersonal dimensions of empathy, respect and genuineness are critical to effective helping.

Truax, C.B. and Carkhuff, R.R.
**Toward Effective Counseling and Therapy**
Chicago, Illinois: Aldine, 1967.

Useful for understanding the historical roots of the HRD models. Presents extensive evidence on client-centered counseling for schizophrenic patients. Concludes that core interpersonal dimensions of empathy, regard and congruence are critical to effective helping.